THE AFRICAN LABOURER

THE
AFRICAN LABOURER

G. St. J. ORDE BROWNE

NEW YORK

BARNES & NOBLE, INC.

Publishers · Booksellers · Since 1873

First published by Oxford University Press for the
International Institute of African Languages and Cultures.

This edition published by
FRANK CASS AND COMPANY LIMITED
67 Great Russell Street, London W.C.1

Published in the United States
in 1967
by Barnes & Noble, Inc.
105 Fifth Avenue, New York, N.Y. 10003

First edition	1933
New impression	1967

Printed in the Republic of Ireland

FOREWORD

IF the treatment of the workers by the privileged classes may be taken as a true criterion of the ethical standard attained by a community, the treatment of African labour affords examples reaching from the era of slavery—when the labourer himself was a saleable commodity—to the spectacle of a standing International 'Committee of Experts' engaged in drafting Conventions to govern the treatment of wage-labour by European employers.

It is with problems of this kind—of housing, diet, wages, the mutual obligations of employer and employed, the duration of contracts, the method of recruiting, habituation, and repatriation, and the precautions needed to avoid the disintegration of native social life—that Major Orde Browne, at the invitation of the International African Institute, deals in the present book.

He is no mere theorist, for as Head of the Labour Department of Tanganyika he has had ample opportunity of putting to a practical test the precepts he advocates. Moreover, by study of the legislation and the practice of the different Governments in Africa, he is able to indicate to what extent they have found it practicable to adopt these principles.

The days of harsh treatment and cruel punishment belong, we may hope, to decades now past. But kind treatment and adequate food are no more than an owner bestows on his domestic animals, or a slave-owner on his household slaves. Something more is required, and the problem of to-day is to ensure that service with Europeans shall not result in the premature disintegration of native society. For the illiterate worker who has lost faith in the approval or the anger of the spirits of his forebears, who has renounced his tribal loyalties and his claim to a share in the family or clan land and the ready help of his fellows in time of need, has now no motive for self-control and becomes a danger to the State.

Should the labourer from a distance bring his wife and family to save him from the temptations and immorality of the labour camp, or will he by so doing sever the strongest of the ties which bind him to his village home? Should the labour-camp with its haphazard congeries of men from different tribes be transformed into an homogeneous model settlement, preserving its accustomed ritual observances, or is such permanent association with an alien race compatible with an evolution which must be gradual if it is to be real and permanent? Can the employers' needs be met, while the labourer learns better methods of life and of agriculture, if the contract does not exceed six months, with compulsory repatriation; or will the journeyings to and fro and the break in continuity of work prove too great an obstacle?

Major Orde Browne's analysis will help the reader to form his own conclusions on these and many other similar problems, the right solution of which will have a profound effect on the future of those Colonies in which large numbers of Africans are employed by Europeans.

LUGARD.

ABINGER
20 *February* 1933.

CONTENTS

CONTENTS

PART I

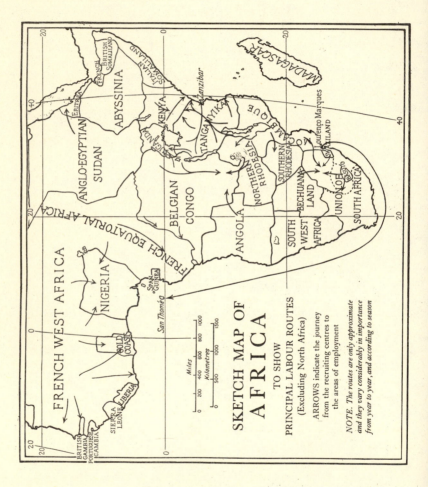

SKETCH MAP OF
AFRICA

TO SHOW
PRINCIPAL LABOUR ROUTES
(Excluding North Africa)

ARROWS indicate the journey
from the recruiting centres to
the areas of employment

NOTE. The routes are only approximate
and they vary considerably in importance
from year to year, and according to season

I. INTRODUCTORY

THE great and growing importance of all problems connected with labour, which has been such a prominent feature in the history of almost every country since the World War, has been as conspicuous in Africa as in any other continent; there, the renewal of the activities suspended during hostilities speedily produced a demand for manual workers that entailed a widespread shortage, and it became increasingly obvious that development must to a large extent be controlled in accordance with the labour available for the various forms of enterprise. Closer attention was thus paid to all aspects of the problem, and innovations of all kinds were introduced to improve the available supplies of labour both in quantity and in quality. Furthermore, in sympathy with the ideals which had found expression in the formation of the League of Nations and the establishment of the Mandate system, there was a strong philanthropic movement towards amelioration of the circumstances of employment. These influences, acting independently but concurrently, produced a rapid advance in knowledge of the difficulties and complications to be faced, and labour administration in all parts of the continent made considerable progress.

The subject, however, has hitherto lacked treatment on a broad basis, and research work has too often tended to be parochial in scope and myopic in outlook. Most valuable information has been accumulated, and data of the highest importance collected, but in almost every case these refer to the special requirements of one particular country, either from the industrial or from the sociological point of view; the comparative study of the whole problem in its present form in various parts of Africa, with the developments to be expected, and the interrelations resulting, has passed generally overlooked.

The upheavals and readjustments consequent upon the Great War are far from finished, and Africa has been as profoundly affected as the rest of the world; instead of regular and progressive development of untapped resources, existing enterprises have been rudely shaken by the factors which have threatened the whole fabric of the capitalist system. The needs of the world, however, remain as great as ever, and the economic exploitation of humanity's untouched assets must progress whatever the system of control. Temporary restriction and stagnation will render the return to activity an increased strain on the social fabric, and there would appear to be a genuine danger that industrial progress may outstrip administrative measures, with possibly disastrous consequences. There is thus a real need for some comprehensive study of the African labour situation on the widest possible basis.

For this reason, the International Institute of African Languages and Cultures has adopted its 'Five Year' Plan, which is intended to form a programme of investigation of the various influences now at work in Africa, with the effects of contact with Western civilization upon native life and character; the present monograph represents one part of this task.

The growing importance of labour administration in Africa seems frequently to be inadequately appreciated; some governments are still inclined to ignore the problem until it is forced upon their notice, while many employers complacently consider an adequate supply of workers the only point of interest to them. Labour is still widely regarded as being merely a department of native administration, meriting no special attention or consideration, and requiring no specific machinery to observe and deal with it; even in countries where paid employment is advancing to a dominating position, it is possible to find reports from medical and educational departments, and publications by missionary societies, in which the obscure and sinister potentialities of the wage-earning system are almost ignored.

The schoolmaster is endeavouring, too often with but moderate success, to train a small proportion of the youth of a tribe, while far greater numbers of the younger adults are receiving a rough-and-ready education in the rude school of industrialism; the doctor does something to mitigate diseases and combat child mortality, but it may be in a group whose whole physical welfare is being jeopardized by conditions of work; the administrator builds a system which, whatever its form, will meet its most severe testing from the returned worker; and the missionary strives to propagate his ideals in the face of a rising tide of scepticism and contempt for authority. From an economic point of view, the reports of companies and industrial undertakings usually refer briefly to the adequacy of the supply of workmen; little attention is paid to the mentality of those labourers, though changes may be occurring which might threaten the very existence of the enterprise. Concerted action by all concerned, with adequate study of the results obtained, is so far rare; the future may be relied upon to demonstrate its desirability.

The complexity of the investigation is as great as its importance, and the sparsity of existing material renders the task more difficult; while comparative studies are available in ethnology, history, language, and other subjects, modern industrial development and the effect of its impact on Africa seem to have received little attention. This work is an attempt to bring together the existing data, and to present the problem in its various aspects, in the hope that the result (however inadequate the accomplishment may prove) will be of service to those responsible for the administration of African labour, whether in a public or a private capacity. The examination will be confined to facts and experience, as far as is possible; no political, philanthropic, or religious standpoint will be adopted, and only an impartial record and forecast will be attempted.

Conditions in North Africa, with the early history of Carthaginian and Roman influence, and the marked difference between Egypt, Tripoli, or Morocco, and the rest of the continent, have made it seem advisable to restrict the area dealt with to the central and southern portion; in other words, the natives dealt with will be principally those usually termed Bantu, with some attention to the west coast in addition.

While the present examination will be primarily directed towards the existing situation and its possible developments, reflection will show the necessity for adequate attention to the historical aspect; the African has been profoundly modified by his contact with other races, and some consideration of these influences and their effect upon his primitive culture and mentality will be essential for any comprehension of his behaviour and reactions. The native is often said to be incomprehensible; possibly a better knowledge of the events and influences which have led to the existing situation might render the remark rarer. The idiosyncrasies of the various European nationalities as wage-earners must be carefully considered by employers; the African will equally repay investigation.

An effort will therefore be made to consider the primitive state of African society, with those characteristics which are most influential in affecting the reaction to modern industrialism; some account will be given of the various forces which have impinged upon and modified this primitive society, and a summary of the history of labour-control in Africa will follow. The subsequent parts of the study will be devoted to a survey of the present position, with some attempt to forecast possible developments.

II. PRIMITIVE AFRICAN SOCIETY

WHILE the conditions existing among the different African tribes before the dawn of history doubtless varied greatly, it is nevertheless possible to attempt a generalized summary of the main features; from this may be deduced the characteristics produced by the old social system for analysis of their effect upon the reaction of the present-day native to changed conditions consequent upon the impact of modern Western civilization on primitive culture.

The original tribes consisted of course of the three groups, hunter, pastoralist, or agriculturalist, with a tendency to progress from the first to the last; instances of all three states are still to be met, though the hunter finds it increasingly difficult to survive. Various influences acted upon each tribe, tending to cause a change in the mode of life; an epidemic might weaken the fighting strength of one, with a consequent loss of security for fields or herds; the rise of a military leader might enable people previously earning a precarious living to subsist largely on the loot from their neighbours; or the hazards of nature, such as drought or pests, might enforce migration and change of mode of life. Prominent among the last must have been that dominating factor, the tsetse fly, with its constant pressure on the pastoralist towards agriculture. It seems certain that tribal moves were by no means uncommon, while profound and far-reaching changes arose from the activities of warlike peoples such as the Zulu. The African thus had a considerable measure of adaptability forced upon him, a characteristic which he retains to a greater degree than is generally recognized, and this must be a valuable asset to him in his efforts to conform to the requirements of modern life.

Turning now to the organization of society, certain features will be found to be common to most tribes in their original state. Law was civil rather than criminal; marriage, like murder, was regarded as the removal of a social unit from the group, thus requiring compensation; useful occupation was the justification for land tenure; mutual aid with food, shelter, or protection was the rule of the tribe, with its concomitant generous hospitality; and the authorities, whether chiefs or elders, received unquestioning obedience.

Routine duties were definitely allocated, and each person had his or her clearly defined position in society. To a greater or less degree, according to circumstances, the younger men were the defensive or offensive force of the tribe, though in many cases they also undertook heavy work, such as hut- or boat-building, tree-felling, or clearing of ground for agriculture. The women were housekeepers and, in addition, did the lighter work on the crops in the case of agriculturalists. Boys herded the cattle or goats, while girls helped their mothers; old men heard lawsuits, while old women helped in the house of their protector. Women were minors throughout life, a nominal 'wife' being thus often only a female relative whose husband was dead.

Society was divided as a rule into clearly defined age-groups; the attainment of puberty was attended with important ceremonies, and the subsequent status of the individual was often marked by further formalities; usually a certain tie between all members of an age-group was recognized.

Numerous other features might be detailed, such as the laws of inheritance, the occurrence of exogamy, the belief in, and resort to, supernatural aid, and so forth; these factors all affect to a greater or less degree the behaviour of the African in modern conditions, but are too elaborate in their nature to admit of any close examination. It will thus be sufficient to emphasize the complicated organization to be found in most tribes, and the consequent continual guidance of each individual by the dictates of custom.

It must be obvious that such a social structure would tend to stress the importance of the welfare of the tribe rather than the individual; each person learnt to think of himself more as a unit in a group than as a separate entity, and he relied with full confidence on the help of that group in case of adversity. When confronted with the unexpected, he depended upon the general consensus of opinion whenever established custom failed to guide, and in deciding upon any enterprise, he acted only after full consultation with his fellows, with a view to combined action. Obedience to tradition was largely maintained by the watchfulness of companions who would protest against the possible injury to the tribe were ancient observances or prohibitions neglected.

In numerous ways the primitive tribesman found himself part

of an organization without which he was lost. Various accidents might make him accursed or unclean, and then he needed the help of the functionary who could remove the consequent danger; without such a remedy, he might suffer the dread penalty of being ostracized by his companions owing to their fear of sharing his supernatural punishment. Members of other tribes could be of little help in such a case, since they observed different rules of conduct, their doctors therefore being unorthodox. Again, the division of duties was frequently upheld by penalties, so that food cooked by the wrong person might entail some social disability if unwittingly eaten; while various articles of diet were to many tribes prohibited and unclean, so that the preparation of a meal was to be entrusted with confidence only to a fellow-tribesman.

The primitive African was thus to a marked degree dependent upon, and influenced by, his companions; crowd psychology thus dominated behaviour, and the individual separated from his fellows was liable to great instability of conduct. This feature was enforced by the circumstances of tribal life where solitude was very rare; almost always in the company of friends, the African had little incentive to the evolution of personality, and remained an extravert; lack of opportunity for meditation rendered him practical and materialist, except in so far as his misconception of the relations of spiritual cause and natural effect made him superstitious.

His qualities and capabilities were also affected by the milieu in which he lived; without discussing the degree to which these originated, or were produced by, the social structure, certain characteristics should be noted.

The solidarity of society naturally led the African to rely on this to a very large degree; the knowledge that disaster would be accompanied by the ready help of friends and neighbours largely minimized the fear of it, and, in consequence, there was less need to foresee or take precautions against misfortune. The tribesman thus tended to become thriftless and improvident; he lived mainly for the moment, expecting the leaders of the community to make such arrangements as they might consider advisable, and relying confidently on the success of concerted effort to meet calamity, should this occur. Being largely relieved of the results of his own foolishness or incompetence by the generous aid of his neighbours, he largely lost fear of the future.

This short-sighted and improvident attitude towards life remains characteristic even when the conditions which may have justified it no longer obtain; the African is conspicuously disinclined to safeguard himself against possible misfortune, preferring to wait until it occurs before taking steps to meet it. Again, when others are open-handed, it must seem penurious to retain one's gains for one's own use; good luck for one meant benefits for all, even in the case of earnings, and thrift was a most unpopular quality.

So whether it is a question of wise investment of savings, or the division of the food-supply for a journey, the African has the defects of his virtues and usually squanders what should serve him in adversity.

While the foregoing summary is not claimed as entirely applicable to any existing group, it is propounded as an approximation to the original mental and moral structure of most tribes; the characteristics noted must have a marked effect on the development of the African in any new surroundings, and they may be detected in his actions in many cases where he is confronted with changed conditions.

The history of the race has provided a considerable amount of material for study of its reactions in unfamiliar surroundings; the enormous slave populations which came into being in many countries have served to show in their varying circumstances how adaptability has been displayed. Transported from his own country, the black man clung tenaciously to many of his old customs, and even implanted them in the new soil; fetish rites have not yet disappeared from Haiti, and the Indians of Mauritius may be heard repeating in French Creole the riddles brought by their slave predecessors from their distant homes. If material vestiges of this type are to be found, it seems certain that the accompanying mentality must also survive to a considerable extent.

Where the African has been in contact with civilization for some generations he has had opportunity to display his aptitude for various activities. Generally, he has shown himself an able orator, and has proved his ability to produce literature and music of high standard; in less intellectual pursuits he forms a useful artisan, an excellent domestic servant, and a capable agriculturalist. In science and business he has not been conspicuous, though he has made some progress in the United States; but many negro-controlled organizations have proved weakest on their financial side.

In government he seems to be distinctly lacking in capacity

when entirely free from European control or advice; Liberia, originally established for freed slaves, and Haiti and San Domingo, which won their own independence, can scarcely be regarded as successful.

It would seem therefore that the old racial characteristics are of durable quality; where the African has had opportunity to develop on European lines he has displayed very much the abilities and weaknesses that might have been expected; presumably, then, similar tendencies may be expected as he progresses in his own country.

III. FOREIGN INFLUENCES

IT will now be necessary to review the influences which have operated in the past to modify profoundly the whole outlook of large sections of the peoples of Africa; for centuries past various elements have been at work to break down the primitive social scheme, and in many cases to cause important changes. As these all serve to indicate the nature of the reaction of the African to alien innovations, and his consequent change of outlook, some consideration of them should be instructive, with a view to deductions applicable to present conditions.

The structure of primitive tribal society had in itself much to be said for it, and as an experiment in government must be considered a decided success in its elementary degree. It can be claimed that the system produced a community where crime was rare, pauperism and paid prostitution unknown, and drunkenness not a serious evil; where, under normal conditions, all were adequately fed, clothed, and housed, according to the primitive standard expected; and where life could be carried on in wholesome and natural circumstances.

Its outstanding weakness, however, was its vulnerability. Internally, it had little stability if faced with war, pestilence, or famine, while local tyrants might at any time obtain undue power; there was also the constant presence of the wizard and his concomitant maze of ritual observances and supernatural claims, often of baleful nature. Even more disastrous was its entire inadequacy for resistance to incursions by invaders possessing greater technical and military knowledge; brute force and primitive weapons could offer no permanent defence against the superior equipment and organization of the older peoples, and an elementary society, with its simple needs, was inevitably attracted by more elaborate artifices, whether beneficial or otherwise.

From very early times, explorers had pushed down the coast of Africa, and Carthaginians and Persians had visited the western and eastern seaboards; the latter indeed had established themselves in considerable towns. Of far greater moment was the Arab invasion which followed the rise of Islam; the stimulating effect of religious enthusiasm led to enterprises by land and sea, prominent among which was the advance down the East African coast.

The introduction of firearms had greatly increased the offensive powers of invaders, and the much-valued ivory of Africa formed a strong incentive for expeditions; thus there grew up at Zanzibar and other points along the seaboard an active and enterprising community which was constantly striving to push farther into the heart of the continent. The carriage of the heavy tusks and the supplies necessary for lengthy journeys entailed the use of numerous porters, and these could obviously be most easily obtained by the capture or purchase of men from the interior; these could then be sold as slaves when they had served their purpose for the journey to the coast. From this, to a regular trade in humanity, was an easy step.

Certain of the truth of their Prophet's revelation, these invaders were filled with proselytizing zeal, and the doctrines of the Koran were spread by the sword. Essentially democratic in character and recognizing no limitations of colour the creed of Mahomet impelled its adherents to the conversion of Africa, a task both meritorious and profitable. Servitude of the body was justified by salvation of the soul, and the cruelties of slave-raiding became the inevitable accompaniments of missionary endeavour. Domestic slavery thus appeared in the country in addition to the former bondage of war captives, and the African entered on his long-drawn-out thraldom as human merchandise.

In this connexion the particular standpoint of Islam is of importance, since it went far to mitigate the lot of the slave. The only division recognized by the conquerors was the religious one; unbelievers were all accursed, but, once converted to the true faith, they became brothers, oblivious of colour or nationality. Thus the slave was compelled to adopt the new creed, but he then became a member, even if a humble one, of his owner's household. He was guaranteed certain rights, his good treatment in sickness and old age was inculcated, and it was a meritorious act to grant his freedom. A female slave bore to her master only free children, and a definite bridge between the two races was thus set up; intermingling became increasingly common, until the line of demarcation between the races grew vague. This must have gone far to enable employer and labourer to understand each other's standpoint, and it may well account for the still existing readiness with which the African will work for the Arab. The horrors of the raids which lined the caravan routes with bones, and filled the markets with bewildered captives, can hardly be exaggerated; once accustomed to the new conditions, however, the slave was probably not very unhappy, while those born in servitude were no doubt in many cases well satisfied with their lot.

The early settlements on the coast were presumably content to carry off members of tribes living near them, and it seems unlikely that raids far inland were attempted to any great extent before the nineteenth century. By that time the trade had become most lucrative and was thoroughly well established.

The Arab communities no doubt established trading and other relations with neighbouring tribes, in addition to slaving and ivory seeking, and in this way they must have formed a source of innovations which were constantly spreading. In very many ways the Arabs differed materially from the African, and new ideas on various subjects would be introduced. Private property not only in personal possessions, but even in land and human beings, must have been a puzzling conception to the Bantu; while the use of money must have appealed to him as an immense boon. A different law of inheritance and a new idea of the status of women and the institution of marriage would also have proved interesting; and, in general, the individualistic outlook, as compared with the old communal attitude, must have been entirely novel.

Thus the first experience that the African received of working regularly for another man was in the form of slavery; previously accustomed to supplying only his own needs, with a share of those of the community, he now encountered a system wherein he was required to toil for the enrichment of one individual who assumed proprietary rights in him; he had, in fact, met the employer though not the wage-payer.

As always in the case of forced labour, the worker was most inefficient unless closely supervised, and this was not to the taste of his easy-going Oriental master; probably only a very moderate standard of performance was exacted, and conditions of life were quite tolerable. Labour was plentiful, and production was not for definite cash returns, so there was little incentive to increase efficiency. It was the master's part to provide food and all other requirements, and to care for the sick and aged, and the slave was thus freed from all responsibility or anxiety. Under a rule in the main kindly, even if occasionally ferocious, he lived entirely in the present, without any incentive to industry, enterprise, or forethought.

The system accorded well enough with African mentality. Sheltered from most misfortunes, except those occasioned by the master's wrath, he led a congenial, carefree life; he was certainly infinitely better situated than his brother in European hands. The greatest injury inflicted on him by it was the mental state which it produced; the very features which rendered it tolerable to him were those that demoralized his character. Sly evasion was his attitude towards a task in which he had no interest, and he received a prolonged education in reluctance to work; his weak points of irresponsibility and lack of forethought were cultivated, and there was little encouragement for the evolution of individuality or character.

When, therefore, people who had acquired this mentality were confronted by the prospect of free labour for wages, they were certain to prove unsatisfactory; they had been taught to shirk, not to work, and found it very difficult to absorb the idea of labour for another combined with profit for oneself. The ex-slave is thus frequently incapable of providing even for his own requirements, and he forms a most discouraging type with which to have any dealings.

This attitude spread also to the tribes living near the Arab settlements; in their dealings with the new-comers, they saw most tasks being performed by their unlucky brethren who had lost their freedom; punishment of offenders and the hunting of runaways would serve to emphasize further the degraded position of the man who had to work for another; so that wage-earning, on its appearance, could expect no favour.

A subsidiary aspect of the Arab slave trade was the initiation of the African into the system; subordinates were wanted for the raiding expeditions, and allies among the native tribes were useful sources of additional numbers. Thus the institution spread and became established among people who had previously only known it in the far milder form of war captivity; the seizure and sale of prisoners became the practice of many chiefs, and some tribes became stalwart supporters of this traffic. In particular the Yao of Nyasaland stoutly resisted early efforts to put a stop to slaver activities in their neighbourhood, and the prolonged resistance of the Arabs of the Congo must have been greatly sustained by native help.

Slavery thus demoralized the society in which it existed, and those tribes which experienced it will usually be found to be most unsatisfactory workers. This, however, is the economic view; from the aspect of the establishment of any colour bar, the Arab influence had little effect, nor does it appear to have made the slaves as a whole embittered or dangerous, at any rate to the degree exemplified by the risings of Africans against their European masters in Haiti, Jamaica, and elsewhere.

IV. FOREIGN INFLUENCES (*continued*)

THE Arab power on the east coast was long established when, in the sixteenth century, the European first made his appearance in equatorial Africa; events in the northern continent had led to this development.

The fall of the Byzantine Empire and the consequent domination by the Turks of the Suez route to the East had entailed the serious curtailment of the valued supplies of spices and other Oriental commodities which had long been appreciated in the West; it therefore became highly desirable to discover an alternative route to Asia, and the sea offered the best prospect for this. Venice, Genoa, and central Europe were involved in the struggle with the Turk; England was exhausted by the Wars of the Roses; France was only just emerging as a united kingdom under Louis XI, while the Netherlands were engaged in a struggle with the Empire. This left the field open to Spain and Portugal, favourably situated on the Atlantic, and vigorous after recuperating from their efforts to expel the Moors. The introduction of the mariner's compass had greatly facilitated navigation, and the possibilities of oceanic exploration were generally favourable. The two Iberian powers were thus able to secure a start in the new trade with the East by sea, which they were to retain for a long period.

Vasco da Gama's rounding of the Cape had been followed by rapid development of the new possibilities, while favourable trade-winds between Spain and South America rendered it easy for that power to exploit the riches to be found there. Friction having arisen between the two nations over their respective activities, the intervention of the Pope led to a virtual settlement, and Portugal, except for Brazil, specialized mainly in the East Indies, Spain putting her energies into South America, except for a few insignificant pieces of Africa.

The great length of the voyages thus entailed introduced fresh complications into the problems of navigation; the small, cramped wooden vessels produced intolerable conditions among the crews, and the resultant sickness and mortality were alarming; scurvy in particular became a scourge. In addition, the unprotected wood of the hulls soon collected a hampering mass of weeds, while marine creatures destroyed the solidity of the timbers. It thus became essential to maintain halting-places *en route* where sick crews could be refreshed and ships careened; Spain established herself in the Canaries, in the fairway to South America, while Portugal for the longer voyage to the East Indies created bases in West and East Africa as well as India. On the west coast there was no great opposition to be overcome, and the colony of Angola was thus early instituted. On the east coast, however, the Portuguese encountered the fierce and powerful opposition of the Arabs established there, who viewed with jealousy the dangerous competition of these formidable unbelievers. The history of the east coast thus becomes for several centuries the story of the swaying fortunes of these two antagonists.

Originally established as posts on the way to the East, the various colonies soon began to display advantages of their own, and development was pushed ahead. This entailed a need for labour on a large scale, and inevitably a resort to slavery followed; at first utilized for local requirements, this soon became of value overseas, and a rapidly expanding export trade in black humanity sprang up. The drain on the manhood of Portugal which resulted from their immense foreign enterprises was to some extent replaced by imported slaves, while Spain required the sturdy African in her South American colonies, where the local natives inconveniently died when forced into servitude. Thus the new possessions gained increasing value as a recruiting-ground for the growing needs of the overseas enterprises.

This type of exploitation had something of the characteristics of the Arab invasion, in that the religious motive was strong; ardent Catholics, both Spaniards and Portuguese carried on a campaign of proselytizing, reinforced by the Pope's demarcation of their respective spheres of influence. Each expedition that left the shores of the mother country was accompanied by parties of priests and monks, and again the forcible conversion of the captive was held to justify his enslavement. The Roman Empire had been singularly free from colour or racial prejudice, though resorting widely to slavery; this view had been largely retained by the Latin nations, but in the case of the Spanish and Portuguese the religious element had been introduced. A bar was thus established, not by colour or race, but by the test of creed; once a good Catholic, the convert was largely admitted to the rights of the national. Interbreeding was not discouraged, nor was the half-caste despised; indeed, colonists would often send their coloured children to the home country to be educated.

There was thus a link between the races, not so strong as in the case of the Arab, but still sufficient to form a bridge by which the subject race might hope to raise itself. This no doubt largely accounts for the fact that slavery under the Latin races was as a whole never so harsh as it was when practised by the northern peoples. While no very definite ideas of policy seem to have been evolved, the general tendency was to consider the African as a degraded and backward heathen, who was to be encouraged to adopt European ideas and standards, thus in time qualifying himself for equal status. This attitude has by no means disappeared, and must be borne in mind when dealing with labour in the colonies of the Latin powers.

After many years of untrammelled power across the oceans the two pioneer nations found their claims disputed. Events in Europe had rendered it possible for competitors to demand a share in the lucrative trade in humanity, and there was a general awakening to the value of the African territories. The conquest of Portugal by Spain in 1580 weakened both nations, already somewhat exhausted by their great colonial activities, while their rivals were rising in power. The Netherlands had freed themselves of Spain and the Empire by the Treaty of Westphalia in 1648, England had become united and enterprising under the rule of the Tudors, and France was rapidly growing in power through the effective combination of kings and ministers who ruled her. The Dutch, in particular, were active in their efforts at expansion in the East; possessing a fine fleet, with daring and hardy seamen, they were determined to grasp a share of the wealth from abroad. Thus the great Dutch East India Company established itself in the Cape in 1652, much rich territory being subsequently acquired in the Far East.

Simultaneously England began to move; her North American colonies were feeling the need for labour, since the Red Indian had proved as useless as his southern brother had to the Spaniards; Cromwell, by securing Jamaica, had presented an appreciative English market with a source of supply of that novel and attractive commodity, sugar, but the plantations required many hands to maintain them. The early appearance of the English in Africa was thus rather as slavers than as colonists, and they were late in acquiring more than small patches of territory for trading purposes. France was busy with her Indian Empire, but, having wrested Bourbon and Mauritius from the Dutch, she imported Africans in large numbers to produce her own supply of sugar, while Madagascar also claimed attention.

Other powers showed slighter interest; the Danes had gained some small West Indian islands, and had secured a footing in West Africa; Austria had interests in the north of the continent, where the Maria Teresa dollar is still current in Abyssinia; Germany and Italy, riven into numerous dissentient petty states, could take no part, and lethargic Russia was too much occupied with discovering her own resources to wish for overseas opportunities.

Unfortunately, all this activity led to the slave trade becoming both greater in importance and far worse in type. The perpetual need for more labour for the American colonies and the terrible mortality among the wretched captives while being established there led to a constantly growing stream of human chattels crossing the Atlantic. The Treaty of Utrecht, in 1713, gave England the right to export 4,800 slaves annually to the South American colonies, though this must have represented a fraction only of the total traffic. The trade became a recognized business, numbers of ships being wholly occupied in it, while large fortunes were thereby made.

The participation of the northern nations introduced a new and far worse character into the relations between black and white. At first there seems to have been little prejudice against a negro in England, and Samuel Pepys was apparently able to add a coloured cook to his household without any resultant difficulty, but gradually a change arose, mainly through the attitude of the planter element from the West Indies. The convenient doctrine was announced that the black man was the descendant of Ham, the accursed son of Noah, and thus condemned perpetually to be 'a servant unto his brethren'. This view was carried to the further degree of classing the negro with the animals, and not as a human being at all, and this was supported apparently in all good faith by the most respectable people; bishops of the English Church quoted Scripture in its defence, and even some Quakers were the owners of large slave-worked plantations. Protestantism doubted the negro's possession of a soul.

The effect of this doctrine (even now by no means extinct) was immense, and disastrous to the African. No longer was there any connecting link between the two races, and no more was there any obligation to consider the spiritual or moral welfare of the subordinate people. The black man was never to be allowed to rise from his servile state, education was denied to him, and intermarriage was sternly discountenanced; the half-caste was regarded with contempt, and allowed no share of his white parent's privileges.

It is not suggested that this extreme view was universally held, but it was sufficiently general to influence all dealings with the African, while even his advocates were singularly modest in their claims on his behalf. In consequence, the slave codes of the northern nations differ greatly from those of the Latins, and in the former there was a ruthless regard of the African as a mere animal which was not to be found in the latter, of which the code of Louis XIV was perhaps the mildest. Brutal and callous owners could be found in South America as they could in the West Indies, but the official attitude was far different on the whole. The result is to be seen in the merging of the black immigrants with the bulk of the population of South America, as contrasted with the sharp division maintained in the north, the British West Indies presenting an interesting exception.

In South Africa the Dutch maintained to a considerable degree the Anglo-Saxon view of the negro; early arrivals found the natives troublesome and dangerous, and largely destroyed them; subsequently the Kaffir was domesticated and gradually acquired a definite place in the Dutch household, though an entirely subordinate one. The excesses of cruelty to slaves which occurred in America were not repeated in South Africa, but the native was regarded as possessing few rights, and, indeed, as a lower order of creation altogether. The Dutch Church recognized his right to religious teaching, but showed little alacrity in imparting it. The colonist led a hard and dangerous life which left small room for sentiment, and he was, if occasion arose, as ready to shoot down troublesome natives as to exterminate the quagga; given, however, that the negro behaved well and made himself useful, the Dutchman was prepared to treat him with a sort of paternal regard, even if of a rough-and-ready kind. Such ill-feeling as existed between the races resulted probably more from acquisition of land regardless of native rights than from slavery. Intermarriage was regarded with detestation, and the half-caste was disliked by both races.

The foregoing is an attempt to outline the general position in the eighteenth century, when the foundations of European contact with Africa were being completed; the difference between the standpoint of the three alien influences, Arab, Latin, and Saxon, still materially affects the status of the native, more especially in his capacity as worker.

V. THE FALL OF SLAVERY

PUBLIC opinion had altered profoundly in its attitude towards the negro during the course of the eighteenth century, and from being regarded as a perfectly normal and respectable social institution slavery became more and more an object of attack by an increasing army of critics, opposed by the weakening if desperate resistance of the planter slave-owners. The controversy grew in volume and heat, and an abolitionist party became rapidly more influential as the whole subject received public consideration. In 1772 Granville Sharp obtained Lord Mansfield's judgement that the law of England could not recognize the ownership of a slave, and, this point once decided, Wilberforce and his supporters exerted increasing pressure to banish slavery from the British colonies.

The Declaration of Independence of the newly formed United States of North America apparently did not contemplate the black man as human; slavery remained firmly entrenched there in spite of any equalitarian professions. A more startling attitude was adopted by the French Republic, which applied the principles of Rousseau's *Contrat Social* in all directions; the negro was a fellow victim of an oppressive system, to be greeted with sympathy and affection, and the citizen of the First Republic exhibited the same sentiments as those professed by the modern exponent of the Soviet Commune, but with wider opportunities for practising them. Deputations were sent to Haiti and other colonies to proclaim the new doctrines to the slaves, but were as far as possible suppressed by the infuriated planters; the ideals of Paris proved unsuitable for exportation. They did not long survive even at home, and the rising of Toussaint Louverture in Haiti furnished an opportunity for a most scurvy action by Napoleon. Nevertheless, the world had been profoundly shaken by the new ideas, and slavery underwent increased criticism; before the nineteenth century was far advanced the barriers had begun to fall, and abolition was carried out as rapidly as proved feasible in all the British colonies.

With commendable anxiety to inflict no injustice, the English Parliament voted considerable sums of money to be paid in compensation to the dispossessed slave-owners; unfortunately, these proved inadequate in amount and unsuitable in form. It was believed that the interest on the capital thus paid would enable the former owners to employ their ex-slaves on regular wages; it was not realized that the demoralization of servitude would render the freedman quite useless as a worker for some considerable time. Liberation was carried through with undue precipitancy, and an established system of employment, even if an evil one, was wrecked without any adequate means for replacing it. The freedmen proved unable to grasp the need for any work at all, and sank into squalid misery through their incapacity to realize that they no longer had a universal provider in the shape of a master; while the former owners lived for a while on the capital sum paid to them as compensation, and then clung on in poverty to their rapidly deteriorating estates.

In South Africa the Dutch were conspicuous sufferers; already disliking the new British conquerors of the Cape, they viewed the liberation of their slaves as either a piece of disastrous sentimentality or a deliberate plot for their ruin. The money paid in compensation was of little use to them, since it could not create labourers for hire, and the Kaffir did not understand working for wages; so their farms were left without the essential labour. In addition, the sums paid were in most cases much below the market value of the slaves, and a grievance was thus created; in other instances ignorant farmers were deliberately swindled by unscrupulous persons, and reduced to penury. The ill-feeling and resentment engendered at that time has done much to embitter relations between the two white races, and to create a suspicion of any piece of native policy advocated from England as probably unpractical and pernicious.

In the Portuguese colonies slavery was not abolished until much later; the various European powers followed the lead of France and Britain in putting a stop to it in their possessions, but only slowly; it was not until the sixties that slavery finally disappeared in the United States, while it lingered still later in South America. The export of Africans across the Atlantic had, however, been greatly reduced at a much earlier date, though smuggling continued for some time. Early in the century efforts had been made to establish freedmen from America in West Africa; results were not encouraging, and the numbers were never very great, the principal survivals of these efforts being the British colony of Sierra Leone and the Republic of Liberia.

In those parts of Africa which were not under European control slavery continued throughout the century; the Sultan of Zanzibar eventually agreed to abolition in his dominions, and this included the portions of the mainland held by Great Britain and Germany. The action of these two powers in effecting freedom was somewhat different, that of the British being more rapid than that of the Germans, who proceeded on deliberate lines which allowed of the extinction of slavery in such a gradual fashion that it still survived at the outbreak of the Great War. But in each case discretion had been learnt from previous experience, and the dislocation of industry which had occurred in earlier instances was largely avoided. Nevertheless, the same trouble arose from the disinclination of the freed slaves to work for wages, or even to take adequate steps to support themselves, and in consequence a low standard of labour was set up, with an irresponsible and reluctant worker who was most inefficient unless closely supervised.

Smuggling of slaves to the Persian Gulf continued long after abolition, but gradually disappeared, though it is not even now certain that occasional cases do not occur.

The partition of Africa among the various European powers eventually eliminated the slave trade except in those parts not under civilized influence, though the peculiarities of the system as operated under the law of Islam entailed a long survival of individual instances. The Koran provided a sort of primitive Employers' Liability and Old Age Pension, and sick or aged servants were maintained in accordance with its provisions; the freeing of such persons was thus anything but a boon to them, and they therefore in many cases absolutely refused to leave their masters and homes. It is to the credit of the Arab that it can be recorded that this obligation was largely recognized by the masters, though not supported by European law, even in cases where the young and useful slaves had taken their freedom.

Private ownership of human beings thus disappeared from the principal countries of Africa, and an effort became necessary to educate the highly inefficient ex-slave population in the advantages of industry. The difficulty of doing this, and the very low average output of the worker, formed a standing obstacle to progress which still exists to a large extent.

Development had taken place with great rapidity in all parts of Africa during the latter part of the nineteenth century; industrial progress in Europe had created enormous new demands, and attention was increasingly turned to the tropics as a source of raw materials. In addition, South Africa, from being an agricultural country advancing but slowly, suddenly sprang into prominence as an important mining centre; gold and diamonds could afford good wages, and a much higher rate of pay for the native worker resulted. The twentieth century continued the exploitation of natural resources, and mining or planting appeared in almost all countries; the Congo proved to have immense mineral wealth, while East Africa was found to be well suited for rubber, coffee, sisal, cotton, and other valuable tropical products; farming enterprise, both for local and overseas markets, also making its appearance. There was thus a general shortage of man-power, particularly of the higher grade, and development was largely dependent upon the labour-supply available for each scheme. European enterprise was eagerly pressing forward with the task of utilizing the newly accessible lands, but was constantly held back by the lack of man-power; the scanty native population was already well enough off to be reluctant to make any effort to secure further possessions, and there was a general tendency to ignore the dominating law of the relation between the increase of needs and the will to work.

As the more remote parts of the continent began to receive attention, employers came into contact with tribes who had not previously had any experience of organized work, either as slaves or as wage-earners; producing themselves almost all that their simple needs required, they lived a self-sufficing existence that rendered them slow to see any sort of advantage in going to work for strangers in order to obtain goods for which they had no particular use when gained.

Their mentality thus differed considerably from that of the sophisticated peoples who had been long in contact with labour systems of some sort; the primitive tribes had no experience of, and no prejudice about, entering the service of others; they merely saw no point in doing so. Therefore, as they began to need more than their own resources would furnish, they equally began to grasp the advantage of earning the wherewithal to purchase the foreign novelties which took their fancy. The employer was thus dealing with two classes: the experienced peoples who had long been familiar with work for others in some form, but who were too lethargic to undertake it at all readily, though quite appreciative of the benefits accruing; and the primitive tribes who were far more inclined to embark on the novel activity, once they had realized the advantages to be gained, and had learnt what was expected of them. These two classes are still widely represented, for there are large sections of population yet untapped as a source of labour.

It seems advisable to stress the division between these types, since their reaction to circumstances of employment is widely different. The native from the experienced tribe will secure the work that suits him best, leaving a place where he finds the task too strenuous or the conditions disagreeable; he distinguishes, and realizes that some other undertaking may prove more congenial. The primitive native, however, is more critical but less discriminating; he is inclined to judge all employers by his first, and if through mismanagement or ill-fortune his party undergoes a discouraging experience, they will probably return home to give a bad name, not only to the particular place of employment, but to the whole system of going away to seek work. Mishandling in the second case is thus more serious than in the first, and it is a matter of some moment that the two classes should be distinguished for appropriate treatment.

While the lethargy which characterizes many of the dwellers on the coast in certain parts of Africa may be mainly attributable to their former experience of slavery, it should also be remembered that they have long been exposed to greater change and movement than the uncontaminated tribes up-country; it thus follows that they have suffered to a larger degree from endemic diseases such as malaria, hookworm, and the other ailments of the low country. Since these are insidious in their influence, being weakening rather than disabling, it may well be that the lack of energy and enterprise observable is to some extent the result of physical weakness and debility. The progress of medical work on this point may produce results of considerable interest.

While a definite mental state was created by slavery, disastrously surviving its abolition, this was not confined to the worker, for the ex-owner was similarly affected; to a man accustomed to regard work as possible only as a result of compulsion, the change to the wage-earning system was almost inconceivable. So the Arab planter proved in many cases quite incapable of recruiting and managing his labour under the new system, and most uneconomical in organizing it; the inevitable result was a resort to loans, with eventual forced sale. To some degree the European was similarly affected, and the former slave-owner found great difficulty in adapting himself to changed conditions; the modified discipline suitable to free labour was not easily learnt, and the lavish waste of man-power was a habit which clung tenaciously. The efficiency percentage was thus very low in the plantations where the old traditions survived, and this naturally tended to establish the general standard; both employer and men grew accustomed to a rate of output that would have appeared absurdly inadequate in a community which had never had experience of the use of forced labour. Slave mentality thus injuriously affected not only the freedman but also the employer and society generally; its baneful effect in lowering efficiency and sanctioning waste will probably take long to disappear completely.

VI. THE INCENTIVE TO WAGE-EARNING

An attempt has been made to trace the history of the various systems of labour management in Africa, both past and present, and to deduce therefrom an estimate of the native's attitude to wage-earning.

The most practical aspect of this survey lies in the consideration of the various influences which may act as incentives to the seeking of employment; both the quantity and the efficiency of the supply available will largely depend upon the reasons actuating the workman in his appearance in the labour market.

The question has two aspects: there is the initial motive for leaving home, and there is the subsequent encouragement to work well when employment has been found.

Under the slave system the volition of the worker was not considered at all; he was kidnapped in the first instance and subsequently compelled to work more or less hard through threat of corporal punishment. Except when incapacitated, he had a certain value as an animal, and was therefore worth caring for to some degree in the matter of food and housing.

After emancipation, the necessity arose for the introduction of some means of securing a supply of labour without resort to raiding; the offer of wages proved inadequate, since the needs of the native were not sufficiently great to furnish the necessary inducement. Various attempts were therefore made to introduce governmental pressure in some form, so that to the self-sufficing life of the village should be added some requirement which could only be met by work for an employer. This might take various forms; the needs of the local government might be thus met by a levy as a form of tax in kind, or a proportion of the able-bodied males might be forced through their chiefs to go to work with private employers, or heavy taxation might be imposed so as to provide a stimulus, or partial exemption from taxation or duties might be offered as a reward for the returned worker; various other schemes or modifications were also tried. In all these cases pressure rather than encouragement was exerted; conditions of employment scarcely affected the supply, and the employer had little interest in the welfare of his work-people.

The third system consisted in reliance upon the natural motive provided by the increasing variety of imported articles which the native desired; as his need for money to buy novelties grew, so his incentive to go to work to earn it would be greater; there was also the love of adventure and the wish to see more of the world. In this case, however, the flow was voluntary, and the employer had therefore to offer at any rate moderately attractive terms and conditions if he was to succeed in collecting an adequate labour force; so the welfare of the worker was in this way assisted.

An analysis of the efficacy of these systems will show that slavery was open to all the material disadvantages of forced labour in the extreme form. The second system, pressure by taxation, provided forced labour in a far less obvious way; indeed, in the mild form of a whole or partial remittance of tax in the case of the returning worker, the element of compulsion is scarcely noticeable. It exists, however, since if it is effectual at all, it acts by entailing a penalty upon those who do not take advantage of the concession, rather than by rewarding the enterprising.

Such methods of applying pressure have met with criticism on moral grounds; a widely maintained view considers it inadmissable to resort to such practices in order to compel otherwise reluctant workers to come forward. The method is defended on the grounds that the vast bulk of the world's population has to work hard for a living, and that there is no reason why the generosity of a bountiful nature should be regarded as excusing the African from taking his share; work is wholesome for all, and if the black man is to advance and raise himself above his present level, he must be encouraged, if necessary, by some slight pressure, to exert himself and attain a higher level of living. Increasing needs will give him a wider enjoyment and appreciation of life, and he will thus be trained in habits of industry. The importance of teaching the native 'the dignity of labour' is frequently stressed, though probably other races might be found equally deficient in this matter, were they not exposed to harsh economic conditions necessitating hard work. Possibly the system of applying fiscal pressure to the potential worker can be best described as an attempt to introduce by artificial means into African conditions the economic incentive automatically functioning in more advanced countries.

Such considerations, however, tend to obscure the practical side of the controversy; the ancient antagonists, oppressor and sentimentalist, once more overwhelm in their quarrel the reasoned conclusions of the impartial observer.

There can be little doubt that a genuine and natural incentive such as the desire to earn money to buy imported novelties, or to accumulate cattle for a marriage settlement, will produce a keener and more ambitious worker than some artificial pressure which drives him unwillingly out at the behest of a headman to secure the revenue due. Equally, it seems obvious that a man who only remains in employment in order to complete a certain period for partial exemption of tax will be a lethargic and listless worker. Still more will the cruder forms of pressure provide only low-grade workers.

African labour is sometimes described as 'cheap'; in reality it is often most expensive. The return for the money paid, and not the rate of wage, is the true criterion, but this very elementary fact seems often to be overlooked. The outstanding disadvantage of African labour is the necessity for constant supervision if an adequate output is to be secured, and this usually entails considerable expense; it is therefore highly desirable that the reliability of the individual worker should be increased, so as to admit of the reduction of overseeing charges. Thus the greater the natural incentive to work the better the prospect of securing a rise in efficiency and reliability, with consequent economy in salaries for supervision.

If this conclusion be correct, it must be regarded as a standing argument against the advisability of resorting to any of the methods for exerting pressure simply on practical grounds. Instances can no doubt be found where there is much to be said for such measures, and many genuine friends of the native will be found to stress the educational value of these; the matter appears to be one for settlement by individual authorities in each instance. In any case it would be well for the question to be considered without losing sight of the problem of furnishing the best incentive to the neophyte worker.

Another disadvantage of the application of pressure to go to work is that it tends to reduce the interest of the employer in improving conditions; in proportion as he can rely upon a certain supply of man-power, so does he cease to trouble about the welfare or contentment of his people. In the extreme cases, the system will become merely a method of extracting the largest possible amount out of the employee in return for the irreducible minimum of food and care, consequent exhaustion or illness being repaired by the discharge of unfit and their replacement by others. At this stage, the position is far worse than under honest slavery, since there is no longer for the worker even the protection afforded by self-interest in caring for a valuable possession.

Such a result is of course far from being produced by a mere manipulation of tax, leaving the labourer free to seek employment where he wishes in a probably insufficiently supplied market; nevertheless, the existence of this feature is undeniable as soon as the pressure becomes perceptible, and as it is unfavourable to the general welfare of the labour market as a whole, it requires adequate consideration.

How far an alteration of tax will operate to any appreciable degree in increasing the flow of labour from a community is arguable. Probably the first introduction of taxation in a raw tribe may serve as the preliminary inducement to many of them to seek work, but after they have formed the habit it seems very doubtful if a few shillings added to the tax will really influence the decision of many men as to whether they should remain at home or not. The experienced worker will as a rule, if questioned, prove to be aiming at the gaining of a considerable sum; he intends to remain away for a number of months and hopes to return decidedly richer; any reasonable increase in tax thus becomes only a fraction of the amount at which he aims, and it must be remembered that dues can only be raised to a modest degree, or heavy pressure will fall upon that part of the population which is not potentially wage-earning. The shop-keeper, in fact, probably provides a far greater incentive than the tax-gatherer.

There is also the less direct consideration of the effect on trade; increased government demands do nothing to raise the spending power of the native; encouragement of trade, on the contrary, will furnish the desired incentive, and at the same time will stimulate commerce, with corresponding advantages to customs and railways.

It may now be apposite to consider the reasons influencing the native who leaves home without pressure to seek wage-earning employment; the manual worker in mines, agriculture, lumbering, and such enterprises, is under consideration rather than the more advanced, skilled or semi-skilled, who may desire a permanent

situation. The incentives may be classed as follows: tax, tribal
obligations, and desire for imported articles, coupled with a wish
for adventure. The first of these has already received some attention; it may be regarded as generally a subsidiary motive, with a
tendency to decrease. The second, tribal obligations, may be
considered as including the various dues required of the native by
his own customs; most African ceremonies involve payment in
money or kind, and prominent among these is the fee necessary on
marriage. This varies very largely according to the tribe; in some
instances it is scarcely a material factor, while in others it may
almost be said to dominate the young man's outlook. Generally
speaking, it is of far greater importance with the pastoralists than
with the agriculturalists, owing to the facility of transfer of property.
It is closely connected with the whole social system of the people,
and, to venture on a generalization, it seems probable that those
tribes in which the marriage customs are breaking down are
deteriorating. (The tsetse fly by destroying herds may thus have
a very definite, if inconspicuous, influence on the structure of
native society.)

No very satisfactory term seems to have been evolved to
describe in English the property transferred at marriage; the exact
nature of this and its original purpose differ among the various
peoples and are the subject of considerable discussion; the
matter is in any case hardly germane to the present inquiry.
Suffice it to say that the marriage payment, when existing in
full force, undoubtedly serves as a marked stimulus to wage-
earning.

Other minor requirements of native life, such as payments to
doctors, fees at entry into age-rank, possible penalties, and so forth,
according to the practice of the individual tribe, all make it desirable that the young man should accumulate at any rate a certain
amount of wealth, which will take the form of cattle among the
pastoralists; this therefore entails more earning. Provision for the
future is probably scarcely existent as a motive; as far as the African
looks ahead at all, he regards his children as being sufficient
insurance for his old age.

Coming now to the last class of incentive, the desire for imported
articles, this will be found to vary very greatly. The self-sufficing
primitive existence breaks down usually fairly rapidly when the
temptations of strange novelties are displayed, but the extent and

speed at which this will take place may differ astonishingly. Certain tribes appear to have a strong prejudice against foreign articles, regarding the retention of the traditional methods as a point of honour; the great majority, on the contrary, accept with avidity any innovation that may take their fancy. Usually there is some discrimination, and certain articles are readily accepted, while others meet with no favour; the women generally prove conservative, and they will sometimes cling to the implements and utensils of older generations even when imported articles are obviously far preferable from a practical standpoint. There is, however, a conspicuous exception to this in the case of clothes; the substitution of woven materials for bark cloth, skins, or other primitive garments is a course that is usually very early taken. Black femininity seems much the same as that of other races, and a wife's jealousy of a neighbour's finery is often the cause of the husband seeking work. In some parts indeed female fashion seems as definite and as fickle as that of Europe, and considerable efforts must be made by some one to secure the latest modes. In fact, the nature of the women's clothing will often be found a very fair indication of the extent to which the men of the tribe already go to seek work, or may be expected to do so.

Besides cloth, various commodities find a ready sale, though, here again, astonishing differences will be found to exist between tribes. Cooking-pots, hurricane lamps, shoes, umbrellas, hoes, and numerous other items will each be found to be the particular favourite of a certain community; fashion no doubt plays a large part in influencing the selection of the purchase, but there are sometimes sound reasons underlying the fancy; extreme prevalence of white ants at home will justify the popularity of tin boxes, or the rarity of salt in the village may render this a valuable commodity to carry back.

The primitive tribe will as a rule be attracted at first by trifles of little value; a knife, axe, or other useful article may be purchased, but it is often accompanied by a number of quite unnecessary adjuncts, such as shoddy but showy clothing, brightly coloured hats, or toys such as mirrors and mouth-organs. Later, the first novelty of the contents of the store will have worn off, and more sensible things will be favoured; metal cooking-pots have been found superior to easily fractured earthenware, blankets are appreciated, or the attractions of lamps may be discovered.

While seldom to be found in the pack of the returning worker, another item of growing popularity will probably prove to be unaccustomed articles of diet; sugar is liked, and tea seems always welcome, curiously enough, since coffee is so much more readily procurable in most parts. Rice often tends to displace the native grains, even when less valuable from the dietary point of view; other articles of food meet with a measure of success in various parts, while the ubiquitous cigarette secures immediate popularity.

Such considerations are well worth the attention of all who are interested in the labour problem, as well as traders. It might indeed prove a wise measure on the part of an administration anxious to improve the flow of labour from a certain locality to take special steps to encourage traders there by offering them improved facilities.

There is also the question of rendering the conditions of life in employment sufficiently congenial to encourage the recruit to return there again; success in this will go far to control the supply of labour available.

The nature of the employment will largely affect the popularity or otherwise of the enterprise; mining, being hard work under fairly strict discipline, is generally far less popular than agricultural employment; it is fortunate that minerals can usually afford the higher wages necessary as extra attraction. Differences also exist in the various forms of agriculture, according as they are easily carried on or prejudiced by occurrence of minor injuries or other disadvantage.

Conditions of life also have a great effect on the reputation of an enterprise, and consequently upon its success in obtaining labour. Housing, food, medical attention, quick and accurate issue of pay, and many minor features, all go to make a place of employment popular or the reverse; sanitation again, though not directly appreciated by the African, may have an important bearing on the subject, since its breakdown may be followed by an epidemic leading to a panic in the labour force, which may result in the general boycotting of the place for years.

Any wise manager will naturally pay close attention to all these points; indeed, he will not be worth his salary if he fails to do so. There is, however, in addition, the need for public attention to individual shortcomings, since the existence of bad conditions will serve to render not only one employer, but wage-earning in general, unpopular; the bad master is the enemy of the good, and low-grade conditions of employment prejudice the whole labour market. Real practical value thus attaches to regulations maintaining certain standards, inspections, and other measures for guarding against objectionable conditions.

VII. FORCED LABOUR

THE diminution of forced labour for private employers has been traced, and this system may be considered to be discredited and moribund; there remains, however, a very considerable amount of forced labour for government purposes, and the circumstances attending this will merit investigation.

Coercion was resorted to freely by almost all the various administrations in their earlier stages; money was scarce, communications bad, conditions primitive, and natives entirely unaccustomed to wage-earning; a proportion of compulsion was thus almost inevitable. Advancing civilization, however, brought to light various disadvantages from the utilitarian point of view, while a growing body of opinion considered all forced labour morally indefensible. The League of Nations, with its subsidiary organizations, drew attention to the problem, and efforts to abolish all resort to compulsion became general.

The African governments, however, claimed the right to make use of compulsion in emergency, or for urgent work for the benefit of the community, the definition of the latter presenting considerable difficulty.

It will probably be admitted by the great majority of people that a resort to coercion is justifiable in such contingencies as flood destruction, bush fires, or rescue work; transport must also be forthcoming for the administrator or doctor hastening to deal with some critical situation. The justification will not be quite so strong when sanction is sought for constructional projects, even though these may be for the benefit of the community concerned; and the building of railways and similar prolonged undertakings should seldom take place under such peculiar conditions that it is quite impossible to obtain free labour.

That a measure of compulsion is at present unavoidable is generally accepted, and it is considered justifiable when employed with the following restrictions; the workers are to be paid at not less than the prevailing market-rate; they are to be properly housed and fed; they are not to be taken unduly far from their homes; and the period of employment must be limited. The observance of these requirements should present little difficulty, and permission on these terms is adequate for most needs.

Borderline cases will occur, where the local population obviously ought to undertake such tasks as a bridge which will serve to evacuate the produce of their own fields, thus increasing its value; they may in practice agree that the building of the bridge is highly desirable in the abstract, but yet prove most unwilling to furnish recruits. Since there is no urgent need for the bridge, it will almost certainly prove possible to import voluntary labour from elsewhere, but this will mean additional expense for transport and higher wages. Is it then fair to the country as a whole to spend this additional sum on the bridge only because the particular community that will benefit by it refuses to help itself? Perhaps an answer might be found in the view that, if the community concerned is prepared to submit to an extra tax to raise the difference, it is entitled to the luxury of labour imported for its convenience. If, however, they are unwilling or unable to pay for this consideration, the government must choose between leaving them to stagnate without the facilities planned, or resorting to compulsion for their own good.

Similar instances could be suggested freely, and it becomes very difficult to draw a definite line; much must depend upon the view taken by the individual government. The problem is one on which there is a wide divergence of views among the various African administrations; the Portuguese, on the one hand, maintain strongly the justification for conscription for purposes that are beneficial or educative, while the other nations largely rule out the educative plea, and resort to compulsion with reluctance, though the degree varies.

One general exception to the objection to compulsion is to be found in the case of conscription for military purposes; those governments whose nationals are liable to a term of service in the army take the view that if this is admissible for their own people, it is reasonable to extend it to the subject races whom they expect eventually to take a place with themselves in the national organization. The view will be noted as a characteristic of the Latin attitude towards races in tutelage; if they are given the rights of the protecting nation, they must accept the obligations; future fellow citizens in civil life must also be brothers in arms; meanwhile, they are required to submit to conscription, if not for military purposes, at least for equivalent labour.

The temptation to utilize such conscript material for purposes of ordinary labour is obvious; the difference between a fatigue party of military conscripts and a gang of forced labourers will then become vague. The point has received much attention, and presents many difficulties; it appears likely to continue to do so, and nations without the necessity for conscription are thus spared a complication.

The most constant form in which forced labour is to be found is in porterage; this survival is still responsible for a colossal expenditure of man-power every year, much of it under compulsion. The lack of communications and the prohibitive expense of building them in many parts of the country necessitate the continued resort to carriers, and it is difficult to see how this can be avoided for some considerable time to come, at any rate in the backward areas.

Most administrations regulate the use of porters with care, particularly when forced; pay must be at the ruling market-rate, distance to be travelled from home is limited, hours of daily journeys are controlled, and feeding and care provided for; usually some restriction as to the total period of service for each man is included.

In spite, however, of such rules, porterage remains very unpopular as a rule, and it forms a decided burden in the eyes of the native. Considerable discrimination is shown in the attitude of the people, certain types of journey being far more unpopular than others; a sporting expedition will generally prove attractive on account of the supply of meat expected, while the leisurely tour of inspection by an official who is well known is also usually readily attended. Continuous travelling with hard and heavy loads, such as boxes of specie, under the eye of an escort, is much disliked.

As a rule, the more primitive people are the readiest to act as carriers; with increasing development this type of work grows in unpopularity. This is fortunate, since it is in the backward parts that porterage persists longest.

While this method of transport must no doubt continue to exist for a considerable time, in many cases more might be done to diminish it. Apart from the obvious permanent remedies such as the construction of means of communication, much could be avoided by better organization; the careful restriction of forwarding of stores, except those urgently needed, to the months most favourable to transport will do something to reduce the requirements. In other cases, greater resort to pack animals might be tried, though in many instances this is of course impossible owing to the presence of tsetse fly. Coercion might also be avoided in many instances by better preparation for a journey; with sufficient notice it will frequently prove possible to find a section of people at some distance who are not averse from earning a little money in this way, but their employment precludes movement at short notice.

Porterage is, quite apart from any compulsion, a most wasteful and uneconomic method of travelling; slow and expensive for its purpose, it also necessitates making up packages in inconveniently small size and weatherproof covering; the procuring of rations and the provision of adequate shelter for each night also often introduce complications. In addition, it represents the withdrawal of the men involved from more useful productive work; this is specially unfortunate, since carriers are usually most needed in wet weather, which is just the time when they should be employed in agriculture, either for themselves or for others. It should not be overlooked that the summons to carry loads necessitates absence not only for the days of actual employment, but also for the time taken to obey the call, and to return home after employment; in addition, some rest will probably be taken afterwards, so that the total time withdrawn from useful occupation is more serious than would at first appear. It is thus clearly important to take all possible steps to reduce this wasteful expenditure of man-power in all directions; the practice of the Belgian authorities in the Congo, of prohibiting the employment of porters over any route on which other means of transport might be utilized, is worth attention.

Unfortunately, administrative officers frequently lose sight of the undesirability of porterage; they have grown used to it, and the message to some native authority calling for so many carriers is so simple that they fail to make every effort to avoid recourse to this method.

Apart from this instance, forced labour is probably in the great majority of instances intensely unpopular with all administrative officers. The call for it is most unwelcome to the natives of the district, and friction is very apt to arise; the tribal authorities are seldom able to arrange matters so as to avoid accusations of favouritism and similar charges, while the effort to ensure that the pressed men remain at work is a most troublesome one. As work-men again, the conscripts are very unsatisfactory, requiring a great deal of supervision if anything is to be accomplished; their period of service is short, and they can thus be taught little about the task required of them; while excuses or pleas for exemption are recurrent. It may thus be taken for granted that the authorities dislike most cordially any resort to compulsion.

Again, coercion in a district must have a most disturbing effect upon the local labour market; the usual flow of volunteers seeking work will be hindered, while there may be an exodus of men wishing to avoid liability. Employers in the neighbourhood will complain that their people have been seized, while countercharges will be brought that they have numbers of nominal workers who are merely using their names as shelters.

Another form of compulsion which still exists in many parts is the communal obligation; this is commonest in the form of road maintenance, when it usually entails the turn-out of most of the population at certain dates, for a brief period, to do the necessary clearing. This is an old and widespread arrangement, generally based on well-established native custom, and it often works very smoothly; if, however, former native tracks are developed into wide roads for wheeled traffic, the obligation may well become burdensome. Again, while very possibly the great majority of people appear without reluctance, there is apt to be some dissentient, usually a knowledgeable young man, who refuses to take part; the native authorities resent this opposition to tribal discipline, and the question then arises as to how the objector is to be coerced; obviously, general resentment will be caused by his exemption, but he will be a disgruntled and troublesome element in the community; his example is likely to be followed, and the whole system soon breaks down.

Yet another type of forced labour may be found in some parts in the form of a tribute to a chief; ancient custom may dictate a few days' work on his fields or village, probably in return for food or beer, under conditions which make the occasion almost a festival. This may work smoothly enough as long as conditions are primitive; the original intention of the system was presumably to provide the chief with an adequate establishment, and to furnish him with a store for the use of visitors, or the relief of destitution. There is, however, a temptation to extend this voluntary effort to the cultivation of valuable crops for the benefit of the chief's pocket, and at this stage friction is sure to arise. Again the solution would seem to be the gradual commutation of the manual service into a cash payment.

A variation of the chief's right to a supply of labour for his own benefit is to be found in the recognition of his power to call out labour for purposes of public welfare; this is to be met with in a number of countries, and has led to certain complications. When exercised for well-recognized purposes of real benefit to the community, it may prove a feasible and acceptable, if primitive, method of carrying out very necessary tasks. It is clear, however, that the justification of the work will depend on the definition of public welfare; where the chief is the sole judge of this, he will be constantly tempted to stretch the application to cover cases which the bulk of his people regard as onerous and unfair. Again, an over-zealous administrative officer may utilize this source of labour to accomplish works which might otherwise be beyond his resources, or, in extreme cases, the chief may accept payment himself for such labour, permitting it to be used for purposes which could not possibly be regarded as beneficial to the whole community. Such practices must naturally cause friction and resentment, with corresponding injury to the authority and influence of the chief; when the obligation is manifestly unfairly imposed, the loyalty of the people will be strained and the tribal organization suffer accordingly. In such cases it will assuredly be the returned worker, accustomed to receiving wages for his task, who will be the first to complain.

The probable occurrence of such developments is now generally recognized, and the power of the chief is usually carefully restricted to cases where the purpose for which the labour is to be used has received definite and specific sanction; it seems inevitable that this type of conscription will gradually disappear, being replaced by an increased contribution to taxation or local rates.

There is a general tendency for resort to compulsion to be abandoned on economic grounds, but still more on ethical; as a means of remedying a labour shortage it appears likely to fall into disuse except in absolute emergency, while the advocate of compulsion for military purposes, or for its educational advantages, will probably eventually maintain this by regular conscription in the first case, and some sort of apprenticeship in the second.

VIII. ALTERNATIVES TO WAGE-EARNING

WITH reference to the evolution of the African, two different schools of thought may be met with; the view which regards his destiny as simply that of a wage-earner, or the opposite one which would wish him to become a producer of his own exportable produce; in other words, it is a question of European enterprise or native crops.

A considerable controversy has arisen in this connexion, the protagonists of paid employment being accused of wishing to produce a serf population dependent for their living entirely on the goodwill of employers who will be in a specially favourable position to exploit them, owing to their lack of organizing capacity. The advocates of exclusive development of economic crops are assailed as ultra-conservative obstructionists, whose ideal is the fly in amber; they are accused of wishing to deny the native the opportunity to learn from contact with a wider world of new ideas and modern methods, thus restricting him to a very limited range of products, and sacrificing a valuable supply of raw materials much needed elsewhere. Considerable exaggeration is to be found on both sides.

The present study has hitherto been concerned mainly with the wage-earner; it will be useful to consider the alternatives open to the native, and the effect that these may have on the labour market.

It is naturally primarily essential for land to be available for the growing of economic crops; if the native has already reached the stage where he has no access to the necessary fields, he loses the alternative and is to this extent reduced to the 'wage-slave' position. This situation arises, however, to any serious degree only in the Union of South Africa, most other parts still reserving sufficient land for the use of at any rate the greater portion of the tribe, the urban population completely divorced from cultivation being hardly existent.

The villager, then, may decide to grow the usual foodstuffs to support his family and after that to admit of sale in sufficient quantity to bring him in such cash as he requires; this plan is very limited in result, and entails an elementary standard of living.

Alternatively, he may grow some exportable crop, such as cotton, coffee, cocoa, ground-nuts, or other article commanding a ready sale; in this case he may obtain an appreciable sum of money for his produce, which will enable him to buy various luxuries, and become one of a fairly prosperous and progressive community. This is the form usually advocated by the supporters of this mode of life, and it has much to be said in its favour. Such a community will not be exposed to the evils consequent on the work-seeking habit, and will probably remain contented and self-contained in their tribal surroundings, with sufficient means to satisfy the requirements of government and provide for their communal wants in addition. They cannot be accused of failing to take their share of the burden of the world, since they are producing valuable raw material or food which is eagerly sought overseas. It would be unworthy to suggest that advocacy is sometimes actuated by the feeling that such a community will be administered with far less trouble than one permeated by the returned worker.

Stock forms an alternative, the tribe living on the sale of cattle and their products; progressive pastoralists, however, seem somewhat rare, the tendency being to keep large numbers of low-grade beasts for the sake of accumulating them, this form of live wealth making a special appeal to the African.

It is often assumed that economic produce tends to exclude wage-earning, and that a tribe finding itself in a position to secure an adequate amount of money from its crops will take no steps to earn wages. Examination will show that this is by no means always the case; instances are frequent where natives will plant a crop intended for sale, go away to work for a while, and return to market their produce.

The introduction of an exportable product is apt to be followed by unduly enthusiastic planting; the few pioneers make startling profits, and there is a rush to imitate them; the crop fails, or the market price falls, and the resultant disappointment leaves many people very inconveniently situated. If overplanting has occurred to the extent that it has prejudiced the growing of food-stuffs, the community may be in a most awkward predicament. Such lessons are not lost on the African, and he learns to maintain an equilibrium, the exportable article being balanced by a proportion of edibles, while spare time may well be spent in a brief period of going away to work. A tribe in which such a state of affairs exists is obviously strongly placed, and unlikely to be seriously affected by disaster.

The opening-up of fresh areas by railways or roads is sometimes regarded as a threat to an existing labour supply, the idea being that the improved facilities for getting away any economic crop already grown will be so great that an enormous increase in acreage will take place, the people gaining so much money in consequence that they will no longer feel any desire to seek wage-earning employment to supplement their incomes. Plausible though such a view may be, it does not appear to be substantiated by experience. The coming of the railway certainly facilitates the getting away of native-grown crops, but this means that the immense amount of time formerly wasted in porterage will be largely economized; buying centres will be established near the areas of production, with motor transport feeders to the railway, and the formerly isolated grower will find a purchaser near at hand. So the four or five loads of raw material which formerly necessitated weeks or even months of weary human transport are now marketable with very little effort; increased crops can be grown, and still the owner will have additional time to spare. The effect in practice of such development is thus to facilitate the better use of energies; wasteful porterage is replaced by productive activity. In addition, the railway will greatly decrease the hardships of the journey to seek work; men accustomed to a long and arduous march will find recruiters ready to offer them attractive contracts with free transport between their homes and the place of employment; this again saves much time formerly wasted. The most recently built railways in East Africa and the Congo provide instances where areas, formerly producing a modicum of economic produce as well as labour, largely increased the output of each when travelling facilities improved. There is also the factor that advancing prosperity produces a general awakening; people become more enterprising, and there is a stimulation of all forms of activity. Where, however, the newly developed area admits of white settlement, an increased demand for labour will naturally follow.

There now arises the question of the best form of enterprise to advocate in a backward community who are just beginning to progress; the administrator will have to decide whether he will urge the ambitious to satisfy their needs by seeking employment, or whether he will introduce some economic crop which appears to promise adequate profits. The employers of the country will favour wage-earning; the advocates of home production will recommend agricultural activity.

In such a case it will be well to examine the type of native concerned, for upon this success in either line will largely depend. Certain tribes appear to have a naturally roving and adventurous disposition, which makes them welcome the prospect of seeing the world and visiting strange people and places; others seem to shrink from going far from home, and to be reluctant to accept work for another. Especially will it be found difficult to create any enthusiasm for wage-earning among a tribe which has had any experience of forced labour in any form; the dislike of compulsion outlasts the existence of it, and the man who has once been educated to regard work for an employer as a misfortune will take long to change his attitude. This presumably accounts for the many instances of tribes who are energetic in the production of crops, but who can only with great difficulty be persuaded to accept a wage, even in their own homes; in some cases indeed they seem to contract a sort of obsession, which makes them abruptly abandon even a congenial job near home if they feel that they have worked at it too long. Probably even a limited amount of compulsory porterage for local purposes will have some effect in this direction.

Local conditions will also of course have to be taken into account; an area in which no specially valuable crop can be grown, but which is near some centre of good employment, is obviously an unlikely field for agricultural enterprise. On the other hand, if the tribe lives in unusual climatic conditions—mountains, river plains, and so forth—it will probably suffer severely in health by transposition to work in a different climate; it would then obviously be ill advised to encourage them to appear in a labour market where they will be both miserable and useless.

Such questions having been carefully considered, it will be possible to form some decision as to the best type of activity to encourage, and here there arises a need for great caution. It is presumed that the administrator has no special interest or pressure to compel him to recommend any particular type of activity, but that he is free to use his legitimate influence to encourage what appears to be the most useful line of advance for his people; he will be well advised to proceed carefully.

An urgent need for labour on some nearby enterprise may furnish an obvious outlet for the energies of the tribe; the conditions of employment may be inspected with care and prove to be unexceptionable; the rations provided will supply a valuable supplement to the scanty diet of the villages, and the medical attention available while at work will prove a great asset in combating preventible disease. Employment in such circumstances would thus seem to be of real benefit to the natives, who are encouraged to go out in large numbers.

It may, however, prove that the peculiar individual susceptibility of the primitive African renders the tribe extremely liable to some ailment; they are, in fact, physically unsuited to the new locality until carefully acclimatized. If, then, crowds have been recruited and sent to work without adequate preliminary investigation, there will almost certainly be a serious outbreak of disease, possibly attended by a high mortality. Both employers and recruits take alarm, panic measures are adopted and possibly the whole force is repatriated hurriedly; the survivors arrive home emaciated and miserable, to spread alarming descriptions of the fate that awaits the work-seeker, and the tribe is thoroughly warned against any future enterprise on such lines. The employers have been put to great expense, and have had to face an ugly record in health returns, so they equally determine that these people must never be tried again. The tribe considers the administrative officer to blame for recommending them to seek such work, and his influence and prestige suffer accordingly; harm has, in fact, been done all round.

Probably had the experiment been conducted with due caution a very different result might have been obtained; a small party might have been recruited under special conditions and set to work under close supervision; the medical staff could have watched them carefully, with a view to detecting and combating any appearance of disease; if necessary, a special diet could have been provided, at any rate at first, and in this way it might well have proved possible to acclimatize the newcomers to unaccustomed conditions, so that, with the experience thus gained, further batches could have been absorbed, and a position achieved such that the tribe was able to find a ready outlet for its energies, while the enterprise secured useful labourers from near at hand. Numerous instances can be found where tribes at first peculiarly susceptible to illness proved later to be perfectly able to stand the change; apparently it would be true to say that any raw tribe will show a marked degree of susceptibility to disease when first experiencing unaccustomed conditions, but that it may be possible for the same people to be acclimatized gradually until they become normal in resisting disease and thrive in employment.

It is equally easy for the advocacy of an economic crop to result in disaster, and here again caution is very necessary.

Possibly a preliminary agricultural survey has indicated some crop such as cotton, coffee, or other valuable plant as offering great possibilities in the locality; conditions appear generally suitable, the tribe concerned has distinct agricultural ability, and no other equally promising line of advance can be found.

A campaign for the encouragement of the crop in question is therefore launched; seed is distributed, chiefs are urged to explain the possibilities to their people, and agricultural instructors are imported to ensure that the new crop shall be produced under favourable circumstances. The venture may be taken up with considerable enthusiasm in many cases; particularly if there are a few initial startling successes; it is, however, probable that a slight element of pressure will creep in, and that the people will grow tired of the constant advocacy of the new crop, a critical and grudging spirit thus coming into being. If then, while the venture is still novel, there is a failure of the harvest, or if the price falls to a figure that brings in a very disappointing return, there will be general resentment; particularly serious will the position be if the food crops have been allowed to fall below the necessary minimum in the expectation of being able to buy supplies with the money gained from the sale of exportable stuffs; a partial famine will appear, necessitating relief measures, and the people will be very ready to blame the authorities whom they regard as responsible for their troubles. In this instance, again, the administration will have lost influence and reputation, and a prejudice against any novelties will have been created; it will be very difficult to persuade these people to make any further experiments. It is obvious that an adequate food-supply should be the first consideration.

Encouragement of economic crops is often advocated as the best and most natural means of combating the undue exodus of the males of a community in search of work; this is no doubt largely true, but the nature of the crop needs consideration. If the men of the tribe have formed the habit of earning considerable sums in employment at a distance from home, it will be essential to offer them some immediate alternative which will provide at any rate a fairly adequate equivalent for their wages; a one-season crop may do this, but it will be useless to expect early success with a plant such as coffee, where several years must elapse before any returns are secured, considerable work and care having to be devoted to it meanwhile. It is requiring too much of a change in mentality to hope that such an alternative will serve as a counter-attraction in a community already accustomed to hard cash returns for their activities; experiments on these lines will have to be conducted cautiously, on a small scale at first.

It is suggested that great care is essential in arriving at any decision upon the question of the most suitable form of advance for any backward community; strictly limited trials are important, and preliminary inquiry most necessary, if disaster is to be avoided. The physical condition of the people, their mental bent, their home diet, the agricultural potentialities of the locality, available means of transport, and similar factors all require consideration, and when once a course is decided upon the accumulating results should be carefully watched, a task in which not only the medical department but also the local missionaries and traders should play their part.

IX. METHODS OF RECRUITING

THE recruitment of labour is a subject on which various conflicting opinions exist, and about which many prejudiced and
ignorant misstatements have been made. The labour agent is
frequently represented as a completely unscrupulous and wholly
undesirable parasite, who makes enormous profits out of the
cunning exploitation of ignorant natives; he is considered the
modern successor of the slaver, wholly indifferent to the welfare
of his chattels, and capable of any sort of roguery or deceit to
cajole his victims into his power.

In actuality, while labour recruiting undeniably lends itself to
knavery and oppression, there is another side to the question; if
respectable persons are selected for the work, and suitable rules
and restraints govern their activities, most valuable services may
be rendered by them to all concerned. Indeed, it may be said that
the labour agent in some form is indispensable.

Considering first the various forms which recruiting may take,
these fall into three groups: (a) government organization; (b)
associations of employers; and (c) private agents. It will be useful
to examine the nature of each of these.

Government recruiting is often advocated, and by two widely
differing interests; there is the person who regards it as the only
means of securing that the business shall be decently and cleanly
conducted, and there is on the other hand the unsuccessful employer who hopes to see a means of securing a measure of governmental pressure on potential recruits, even if veiled. There is some
reason for both these views.

It is certain that a well-planned official organization, managed
by reputable persons under responsible auspices and without
pecuniary interests in results, will enable the ordinary abuses to be
eliminated to a great extent; as a government department it will
have the support of the administration, and its records and statistics
will be available for official purposes, in itself a great advantage; its
activities can be controlled and its arrangements for the care of
recruits carefully scrutinized. From the employer's point of view,
it should eliminate much wasteful competition and offer its

services at a fair rate, while it will be honest and reliable in its dealings.

Consideration will reveal certain defects that are serious; the extent to which they will appear must vary with circumstances, but they are always a potential danger. The first disadvantage lies in the risk of an element of compulsion creeping in; if the recruiter is a government official, he will always inspire a certain awe in the mind of the native, and without intending to do so he will probably be considered as giving orders when he is only making suggestions. This will inevitably lead to friction between him and the administrative officer, when the local chiefs will not be slow to take advantage of the possibilities of setting one official against another. Again, the recruiter is by the nature of his work peculiarly exposed to accusations, and it is clearly undesirable to have an official constantly liable to be charged by some disgruntled native with resorting to bribery, using threats, withholding money, or the many other complaints that may be brought forward.

The second weakness is that an official service must be available for all; there can be no discrimination between employers, except possibly under clearly defined rules, such as actual convictions recorded. This entails the provision of servants for any applicant, and the bad employer must have as ready help as the good; the agent must do his best to encourage men to go to a place where he privately knows conditions to be bad or at least indifferent, and he eventually finds himself in the position of constantly helping the bad employer, since it is he that will most need the services of the agency. In other words, a government official will be using his best efforts to recommend men to go to low-grade masters, the satisfactory estates having far less need of help. Should the agency fail to furnish the supply demanded by any applicant, there will be an outcry about incompetence or favouritism which the agent will find difficulty in answering, unless he can produce definite evidence, sustainable in court, of bad conditions on the complainant's property. The private recruiter, on the other hand, can discriminate without having to give any reasons, and can merely regret his inability to fill an undesired order, without rendering himself liable to any accusation or inquiry.

It thus follows that a government recruiting agency will tend to become a means of assisting the bad employer, which result is entirely opposed to the interests of the good employer and the native, as well as the country as a whole.

The second form of recruiting agency, the association of employers, is to be found in various parts of Africa; it has much to be said for it, and sometimes seems to work fairly well; there are, however, important disadvantages.

There is usually considerable difficulty in finding suitable men to conduct it; all the exceptional and peculiar gifts of the able recruiter are required, while in addition great tact and patience will be necessary in satisfying the demands of the many members of the association. The periodical meetings at which the recruiter's efforts are discussed will frequently prove to be angry attacks on him by those whom he has failed to satisfy, while others probably know that there was good reason for the failure; some of the members secede, and the organization breaks up.

There is again the weakness that the system tends to favour the bad employer at the expense of the good; some regular contribution will probably be required from each member to provide nucleus working expenses, the recruiter depending on results for the bulk of his salary. But it is quite likely that several popular and important properties do not need the services of the association, and they will resent paying for an organization which exists to help their less capable neighbours; they retire from it and the recruiter finds himself gradually reduced to catering for unpopular employers only; it is a short step from this to the stage where he is shunned by the natives.

Accounting, care and upkeep of camps and equipment, wages for native staff, and similar questions all present sources of disagreement, and in practice such organizations seem to have a short life; there are certain well-established ones, but they are usually expensive and always violently criticized by many.

There is an intermediate type of organization which appears in connexion with very big enterprises; it is a large separate department of the main business, occupied in securing the requisite labour, but working only for the one company. Usually regarded favourably by the government, and very well managed, it forms a sort of intermediate type between the official agency and the private recruiter. Instances may be cited in the Witwatersrand Native Labour Agency and the organization of the Union Minière in the Congo; this type of recruiting is confined to very large companies, usually engaged in mining; it is on the whole very satisfactory, the main objection being the lack of any alternative to its monopoly.

Coming now to the third type of recruiter, the private person, a great variety will be discovered; he may be anything between an unscrupulous rogue who is a public danger and a most reputable person who is rendering a real service to the community.

Unfortunately the astonishing inability to learn by the experiences of other countries which seems to characterize African governments when called upon to deal with labour questions has led to a regrettable neglect of the recruiting problem in its early stages in each colony. There seems to be no instance of a country having foreseen the need for legislation to control labour agents' activities, and matters have been allowed to drift until a positive scandal forced action; even then each government seems to have groped its independent way through a series of rules, growing in complexity as the labour market became more important.

In early days the free and untrammelled recruiter was usually a most undesirable person. He was dealing with ignorant and gullible natives, and possibly inexperienced employers as well; so tricks and deceptions of all kinds were possible. He usually had no intention of establishing a permanent business on well organized and adequately capitalized lines, and he therefore cared little for his reputation. Taking to the occupation as a profitable alternative to big-game shooting or prospecting, he was lavish in his promises to employers as well as natives; so long as he secured a substantial first payment on account for expenses, he troubled little about promptitude in fulfilling orders, and relied on a rapid departure when complaints grew too threatening.

Such a man was of course completely unscrupulous in his dealings with natives. Starting by bribing the chief, usually with liquor, he went on to hold out offers of most attractive wages and conditions to all prospective recruits; utterly incorrect descriptions of work, food, and other details would serve to secure adequate numbers. Some sort of contract usually followed, providing opportunities of swindling the more gullible employers by means of alleged advances of cash and provision of rations. The gangs once dispatched, the employer became liable for final payment on the arrival of his recruits; the subsequent complete disillusionment of both parties when they discovered the degree of their victimization, and their consequent mutual dissatisfaction, left the labour agent quite unmoved. He continued the business until the growing indignation of his clients and his bad reputation among natives convinced him that the time for an unobtrusive departure had arrived; he had put very little capital into the venture, and left behind him only debts.

The harm done by such a man was of course enormous; employers were robbed and furnished with utterly useless labour; natives were cheated and seriously discouraged from further efforts to seek work and, in addition, were rendered suspicious of all promises by strangers in the future; the man was, in fact, a public nuisance of the most serious nature.

The days when such methods were possible have now disappeared; in all countries regulations will be found which prevent the easy issue of a recruiter's licence to any applicant, while in most cases substantial security is demanded, previous reputation and past history also being examined. Methods and arrangements are scrutinized, and the recruiter is compelled to maintain a satisfactory organization open to official inspection.

With such conditions the business can only attract a very different type from the old 'blackbirder'. An appreciable amount of capital will be necessary for the construction of camps and other accommodation; assistants will be required, and a reliable native staff will have to be found. The entire success of the venture will depend upon the extent to which employers are satisfied, on the one hand, and the native recruits are contented, on the other; since the business is intended as a serious one, the permanent and full-time occupation of its owner, any resort to trickery or deception becomes disastrous; the reputation of the concern is vital to its future, and the greatest possible care must be taken to preserve a good name. A dissatisfied client who complains of the type of recruit sent to him will give the agent a bad name throughout a neighbourhood; the inability of the latter to get his final account for the recruits settled meets with little sympathy, and any action against an employer makes the agent a marked man. Even more serious may be the effect of a mistake in dealing with recruits; if a batch is sent to a place where they are ill treated, or where conditions are objectionable, they will return voluble in their complaints of the agent in whose recommendation they trusted. The recruiter may have honestly believed that he was sending the men to excellent employment; they will nevertheless consider him entirely responsible for their disappointment. Even an error in some detail of the contract, such as the exact nature of the work to be done, may cause a gang to consider themselves deceived, and then no explanation will remedy matters. Natives, comprehensibly enough, attach great importance to the personality of a recruiter; if they know him and trust him, they will accept his recommendation of employment quite readily, and he is thus able to supply recruits to new clients without difficulty. If, however, he makes a mistake, and the recommendation proves unjustified, his reputation suffers a severe blow; should other cases occur, he speedily gains a bad name, when his business is automatically terminated, all the capital sunk in it being lost, since no one will take over a recruiting business that has once acquired unpopularity with the natives.

It follows that the recruiter is extremely careful in his work; on one side he must try to find recruits who will give his clients satisfaction, and who can be relied upon to make an honest effort to carry out the terms of their contract; on the other hand, he must avoid employers who may be unscrupulous or ignorant and thus upset his recruits, who will return home to discourage others from going to him. It thus follows that the private recruiter is a powerful supporter of the good employer, unlike the other systems of recruiting previously discussed; he is constantly hoping for orders from the best-managed undertakings, which have good reputations, and will therefore be easy to provide for and satisfactory in their treatment of recruits, but he is unfortunately favoured mainly with applications from unsuccessful employers, among which he must discriminate carefully, lest he send a batch of men to a place which will wreck his standing with his recruits. Since, however, he can easily refuse tactfully, without any need for explanation, he can avoid all known bad employers. It thus happens that a manager with a bad reputation may find that not only do natives refuse to come to him of their own accord but that recruiters seem strangely unable to comply with his requests for men.

It will thus be seen that the private agent, when of the right type and properly controlled, has every incentive to try to satisfy both employers and recruits as far as possible; he is interested in seeing that the contract is honest and accurate, and that in case of any dispute both sides are fairly treated. To retain popularity with his recruits he must provide adequate arrangements for their accommodation and their journey, and he must be prepared to help them in any way in which they require it. He is thus a real influence for improved conditions, and a genuine asset to the labour market.

X. CONDITIONS OF RECRUITING

THE circumstances in which recruiting is carried on are naturally of great importance; not only have they importance for the welfare of the workers, but they have a conspicuous effect on the flow of labour.

Where the work is carried on by a government agency or a well-controlled company there should naturally be no difficulty in exercising proper control or securing the right type of person to manage the business. If, however, the private agent is permitted, certain legal conditions will be found desirable.

The recruiter should be a man of good reputation and standing, having a close acquaintance with the natives with whom he will be dealing; he will also require a sound knowledge of the local language. In addition, he must possess that obscure faculty which can only be described as the ability to 'get on well' with Africans. Some sort of bond should be required of him to ensure that there is a hold over his movements, and to secure a means of meeting any penalty that may be imposed for infractions of law. Rules will be needed determining the accommodation, rations, method of transport, and other questions relating to the welfare of the recruits. Provision should be made for the inspection of camps, vehicles, stores and other equipment by administrative, labour, and medical officers. Adequate book-keeping should be secured to enable the methods of the business to be examined if necessary and to furnish valuable statistics for government use. It will also probably be found necessary to restrict the scope of the licence so as to curb competition, eliminate the recruiting of tribes for any reason undesirable, maintain quarantine, and otherwise comply with administrative demands. A register of the subordinate staff to be employed should also be kept and deposited with the supervising authority, both to ensure that undesirables are excluded, and to protect the recruiter from illicit exploitation of his name by unauthorized persons; it will probably be found of service to all concerned if his staff wear a distinctive badge, and his camps or depots are permitted to fly a special flag, or otherwise proclaim their ownership. This will be of assistance to the recruits, and will in addition render detection of irregularities easier.

The conditions of the journey will vary greatly with the state of transport of the country; rail or motor conveyance will greatly simplify the problem, but these are only to be hoped for in the more developed areas, whereas recruiting will probably take place in backward parts. Marches of considerable length will thus probably be inevitable, and adequate provision is most important; probably the hardships of the journey in this form are one of the principal deterrents of labour.

Whatever the form that recruiting may take, certain requisites should be provided. Camps of sound weatherproof construction will be needed for each night's halt, sanitation receiving due care; the water-supply must be assured, and arrangements for providing food will be needed. In this particular there should be no great difficulty in furnishing the bulk of the ration, but such items as fresh vegetables or fruit may present complications; it is thus well worth while to start plantations of suitable trees near any permanent camps to supply this very essential ingredient of diet. Some sort of provision should also be made for simple medical attention, for a native will struggle to keep up with his party in spite of a sore foot, slight ailment, or other disability, thus rendering it far more serious, whereas attention in the early stages might save much delay and distress. These camps will also provide useful centres for collecting statistics, while a valuable watch can be kept for the appearance of any epidemic disease; permission to use the small amount of land required should present little difficulty, since the camp will relieve the locality of the nuisance of unaccommodated travellers, and thus be popular with the local natives, who will also benefit by the dispensary there.

The issue of rations needs special attention; as a rule it will prove very unsatisfactory to provide each traveller with money to purchase food en route, since the improvidence of the African entails the prompt spending of most of this, a spell of short commons following; also, the purchases are seldom of the most suitable nature. The provision of food in kind is preferable, but here again there is a considerable risk of waste, while it is also impossible to use perishable articles for such a purpose, cooking facilities presenting an additional complication. By far the best system is to maintain distributing posts at each, or every second, night's halts, where the men can be supplied with an adequate ration; this, however, entails the maintenance by contract or otherwise of a chain of stores, and this may be most difficult to arrange. If feasible it should be worked in conjunction with a system of tickets, which can be exchanged, at the particular store indicated, for one complete ration. This simplifies accounting, and, in addition, it ensures that the food is really available where needed, the possibility of waste *en route*, as in the case of money or food carried, being excluded. Again, it helps to expedite the party on their road, since the fact that they have each so many tickets representing a day's food, not negotiable, and exchangeable only at certain camps, will tend to keep them moving along the road to schedule.

Such chains of camps may be maintained by private recruiters, but they are more feasible for the large companies or governments. The Rhodesian Native Labour Bureau maintains such camps, while the main routes of the Belgian Congo and the Union of South Africa also furnish examples; the Tanganyika Government has constructed them at principal points, but the immense distances to be covered in that country have hitherto precluded a complete system being established.

Where more rapid means of transport exist, it is possible to dispense with all but the main camps at the junctions, and these can therefore be better built and equipped; in this matter the Congo is fortunate, as the main labour routes are well provided with facilities; in particular, the specially built steamers on the lakes are worth attention.

As transport improves, it is important to encourage the use of it as far as possible; otherwise the private agent in particular will shrink from the capital expense required to establish his motor service, or will grudge the fare by rail, and will adhere to the old road journey, even though his recruits thereby waste time and arrive in poor condition, which does him little credit. It may thus be useful that government action should be taken; specially reduced fares are granted on most railways for batches of labourers, while it may even be possible to prohibit sending recruits on foot where other means of transport exist, as is done in the Congo.

In any case, it is very certain that the interests of all concerned favour considerable trouble being taken to facilitate the transport of labourers; recruiters and employers both profit therefrom, while the men themselves greatly appreciate any amelioration. Sickness is reduced, travellers arrive in far better condition at their journey's end, waste of time and contract-breaking are lessened, and the government sees its people helped to expend their energies usefully instead of in weary and deleterious marching which is of no profit to any one.

Medical inspection is practically essential in connexion with recruiting, since it is obviously impossible to risk sending a party of men on a long journey, only to find that numbers of them on arrival prove unfit for work. Most governments therefore insist on this, and it is usually carried out free by official medical officers at the first available post. Portuguese law requires inspection both on enlistment and on arrival at the place of employment; the arrangements of the Union Minière and certain other companies secure the same result; this, where feasible, provides a valuable check on the arrangements for the march, and brings to light any instances where the journey is proving too trying. The safeguard of the medical inspection is much appreciated by the employers and by the more enlightened recruiters; even in the case of those governments which still retain some charge for it there is seldom any objection raised.

The advantage of good arrangements for the journey is conspicuous in the case of those tribes which are just beginning to appear in the labour market; these are mostly particularly susceptible to change, and are thus liable to fall sick on arrival or soon after; they have a better chance of growing acclimatized if they arrive in good condition rather than debilitated by deficiencies in food or accommodation *en route*.

The practice of segregating batches of new arrivals in a special camp, where they can be given appropriate food and light work while being kept under medical observation, is becoming increasingly common; it ensures that the best conditions are secured for inuring the recruits to the strange climate and food, while it also enables suitable steps to be taken to deal with any disease that may be found to be dormant in them, such as hookworm, malaria, or other common African complaint. While this is usually done only on the large properties at present, it would repay employers of labour on any considerable scale, since the proportion of subsequent sickness thus avoided will far outweigh any expense or inconvenience incurred.

The task of recruiting is not finished when the men have arrived at the place of employment; the return journey on the completion of the contract is of equal importance. This is usually provided for by law, and similar conditions are exacted as those for the first; whether government organization, association, or private recruiter is concerned, the obligation to the labourer is not discharged until he has been returned to his home. In a well-managed system this should afford a valuable means of observing the effect of their experiences on the men; if necessary, another medical examination can be carried out to provide statistics to indicate the benefits or disadvantages resulting and thus to influence the permitting of further recruiting. Muster-rolls can be carefully scrutinized to secure vital statistics and details of accidents, thus providing a check on the figures furnished by the employer. In the case of the private recruiter, the returning worker will be able to give him many valuable hints for the improvement of his arrangements and the popularizing of his organization, while much useful information may also be gathered about the characters of employers and the standard of work expected.

Whatever the system adopted for recruiting, it is certain that the circumstances attendant on it are of great importance; if the natives are to go to work at all, it is essential that this should be under conditions as favourable as possible, as much from the utilitarian as from the humane point of view. Among these, the ensuring of an honest contract and the securing of decent treatment while travelling have an important bearing on the contentment and well-being of the worker and the healthy condition of the labour market.

XI. THE CONTRACT

THE question of the Labour Contract and its terms is of great importance; it will be found to cover a wide variety of forms, from a sort of declaration of terms of servitude to a charter of the worker's rights. The older and more primitive kind of contract set forth merely the task which would be required of the servant, with details of time, wages, &c., for which he was expected to work; the punishments to which he rendered himself liable in case of any breach of regulations were cited, and the document was made as far as possible a bond which should firmly secure the servant for the whole term of the contract. This entirely one-sided agreement was in fact merely a trap for the worker; he was usually induced to agree to it by some cajolery or trickery, and often without comprehending its terms; he then discovered that he had committed himself to most serious liabilities with little hope of sympathy if he got into trouble as a result; small wonder if he learnt to mistrust all contracts, which thus became generally discredited as being seldom honest documents.

A state of affairs where it became impossible to make any genuine formal agreement about labour was equally inconvenient to all concerned, and it was seen that some better and fairer sort of contract must be introduced in which the interests of both parties were taken into account; an effort was made to secure some advantages, as well as disadvantages, for the worker, who might thus see that he had something to gain by entering into a voluntary agreement. This practical view was reinforced by the growing desire to secure fair play for the African generally, and especially in the matter of labour conditions. It will thus be found that the modern contracts mostly furnish increasing evidence of a desire to provide safeguards for the worker, and they usually define the obligations on each side with reasonable fairness.

A curious feature of the legislation of many countries on the subject of labour contracts is the implication that the employer will always be European, or at least not an African; the old South African Master and Servants Law is reproduced in title in the Masters and Native Servants Ordinances of the British East

African group. The possibility of African employers becoming important seems to have been overlooked, though they already exist in numerous cases; the restriction of the law to 'native servants' has also had the peculiar result of rendering its provisions inoperative in the case of workers other than Africans, with corresponding lack of protection to these in many matters relating to conditions of employment. The various international conventions are also affected to some extent, and it would seem that this peculiar species of colour privilege will be eliminated in future legislation.

The chief points to be secured were that the worker should enter into his obligations willingly, and that he should understand what these were; to attain these objects, the laws of most African countries now provide that all labour contracts are to be approved by an official who shall certify that the agreement was made voluntarily and that he satisfied himself that the conditions were understood by all concerned.

This arrangement in itself should go far to ensure that the recruits are not being subjected to pressure from some source, and that they realize the circumstances in which they will be working; unfortunately, however, there remains a risk that the duty may be performed in a perfunctory manner by a slovenly or overworked official, when abuses may easily creep in; the need for subsequent checking of the terms of the contract by some independent person thus arises. This is met, in the legislation of some countries, by the appointment of special inspectors whose duties include the examination and checking of all contracts held by the workers on the properties which they visit. In other cases such definite provision does not exist, but the need for some such safeguard is recognized to some extent in almost all codes.

The terms of the agreement have also in most cases been subjected to control; security is provided for proper housing, sanitation, medical attention, and similar requirements, while an undertaking to provide clothing, journey facilities, and other advantages is also often included. An important feature of almost every code is the stipulation that wages shall be paid in current coin at specified intervals, thus guarding against any 'truck' system of wages in kind; in some instances payment of wages is prohibited in any shop or canteen as a safeguard against pressure to spend at an establishment in which the employer has an interest, while measures to prevent any similar encouragement of the consumption of liquor should also occur.

The question of 'truck' presents certain difficulties not immediately obvious, and it is possible that in some codes unduly strict regulations against any such danger have been introduced; in particular, the prohibition of any shop or canteen provided by the management for the use of its employees would appear too harsh, though such a rule is to be found. While there is an obvious danger that an establishment of this kind might be made a means of illicit profit through pressure brought to bear upon the workmen to patronize it, any attempt to carry this to a point where the proceeds were appreciable would probably be resented to a degree that would render the employer unpopular, with consequent labour shortage. On the other hand, a large undertaking will generally be able to maintain a store for the sale of all the more ordinary articles at a price below that of the shops of the locality, and, if well managed, such an institution may be a real boon to its customers. It is often difficult to attract any but petty traders to satisfy the needs of a group of labourers, and profits tend to be unduly high, since the restricted market limits competition. It is thus probable that the establishment of private stores for the use of employees will be in the main beneficial, though provision may well be made for supervision of the methods of business to guard against unfair exploitation.

The rule that wages must be paid in cash, at stated intervals, is intended to ensure that accounts are kept up to date, and that no complications calculated to bewilder and cheat the native are introduced; this is of special importance in connexion with the type of shop referred to above, where, if credit be allowed, it may well be possible for a man to fall so deeply into debt that he has little hope of ever freeing himself; if such a system be permitted or upheld by law, it may produce something very like actual slavery, as in the case of the peonage system in parts of America. Certain African countries have a law which prohibits all credit to natives, except with special sanction, and this naturally precludes any hold by the employer on his servant by means of an alleged debt; opposed by many people as a hindrance to legitimate trade, the undeniable benefits of some such provision of the law in the case of a primitive community are so conspicuous as to suggest careful examination of the position in countries where there is no such limitation, not only from the point of view of labour legislation but as a general measure.

Another vexed question is the inclusion in the contract of a
. provision for the retention of a proportion of the wage as a deferred payment, to be made to the employee at the end of the contract, or on his arrival at his home, after completing his obligations. This is to be found in the law of two important labour-exporting countries, Rhodesia and Portuguese East Africa, while it also appears in many codes in other parts of the world.

This stipulation is usually represented as a benefit to the employee; it encourages thrift, it reduces waste of money on gambling or other vices, it ensures a satisfactory lump sum for the worker at the end of his contract, it prevents any risk of theft on the return journey, and it encourages the spending of a fair share of the earnings in the home village.

Another aspect is the fact that the retention of a part of the wage gives the employer a powerful hold on the worker since the contract usually entails loss of wages due in case of breach, though this is generally subject to legal authorization. It is also noteworthy that the countries where it is most prominent are labour-exporting countries; presumably the desire to ensure that a proportion of wages earned are spent in the home country prompted the introduction of the rule to some extent. Countries where such a law might have been expected are Swaziland, Basutoland, and Bechuanaland, none of which, however, has found the obligatory system advisable, a voluntary scheme only being maintained.

While there is no doubt much in favour of encouraging the payment of deferred wages, there is a factor constantly militating against the popularity of any such scheme which is often overlooked; this is the great variation in value of merchandise in the place of employment and in the home village. Usually the recruit comes from some fairly remote locality, where transport charges and a restricted market lead to very high local prices; he goes to work in some far more accessible area, where goods are, to him, amazingly cheap; small wonder, therefore, that he determines to buy as much as possible while at work, with a view to carrying it home for use or sale at a profit. He does not take into consideration the trouble of carrying his bundle for a long march, and merely thinks that he has discovered an excellent way of circumventing the profiteering of the traders at home. He will therefore much resent any system which prevents him from carrying out this manœuvre, and which, for his cheap goods, would substitute the same nominal amount of wages with a greatly reduced purchasing power. This objection, however, applies only to imported goods; the young man · wishing to buy cattle for a marriage contract will benefit by having payment of his wages deferred, as he will probably realize.

The question is one which will probably be dealt with on a voluntary basis in future legislation; legal regulation of such points is likely to lead to increasing criticism and opposition, while most advantages for the employee could be secured by providing him with means for deferring payment should he wish to do so.

A somewhat similar, though less important, problem is the remission of a part of the wage to the relatives left at home; occasionally contracts will specify some arrangement for this, and the point is well worth considering. Most recruits, on leaving home, are much perturbed about the welfare of their families while they are absent, and, in particular, the payment of any tax that may fall due; hence the importance in recruiting of providing for a reasonable advance and the meeting of the tax for the year. This, however, does not fulfil all requirements, and it would often be a boon to employees were they able to remit part of their wages to their homes. Private employers occasionally try to facilitate this, but the machinery for carrying it out is generally lacking; postal orders are liable to go astray or be misused by impostors, while the area of recruitment will also usually have to rely on the services of a small administrative office for any financial arrangements. Any system for payment of deferred wages might therefore well be adapted to provide also for periodical remittances.

In this connexion instances are occasionally to be met with where special arrangements have been made to facilitate the worker's communication with his home; a native clerk is partly or wholly employed in writing letters for a small payment and these are dispatched, intelligibly addressed and containing a sheet of blank paper and an envelope printed with the address of the property. This goes far to eliminate the risks attendant on the usual semi-literate native correspondence, and does much to ensure the safe arrival of the letter with postal order or other enclosure, while it enables the recipient to enlist the services of a friend with a pencil to reply, should he or she be unable to write; the printed envelope only requires the addition of the name of the sender to render its due receipt reasonably certain. Such a service is enormously appreciated by a labour force, and will in itself do much to render that place of employment popular.

The form of the contract varies greatly, though the provisions included in it are usually much the same; it may also be individual, or collective to cover the requirements of a whole gang. Early legislation favoured the large sheet of names which reduced the work involved, and this form will still be found in countries where there is not the necessary staff to give adequate attention to labour matters; recent advance has, however, introduced the individual contract on a widening scale, and it appears likely to become general as progress in such matters is made. The disadvantages of the collective contract are obvious; in particular, it renders action almost impossible in the case of the man who has for some reason become separated from his party, and it is thereby most unjust to the recruit; it also facilitates the decoying away of employees, while it practically precludes such additions to the terms as increases of wages, which are consequently only verbal in individual cases, and it gives the worker no copy of a past contract which he can produce when seeking work again. Its sole advantage lies in the facility which it provides for checking details relating to a whole gang; where health statistics or similar particulars are concerned, the collective contract is a decided advantage; this, however, is also easily achieved by the retention of a copy of the list of recruits which must accompany each batch for the information of the prospective employer.

The number of copies of contracts required by law varies greatly; obviously the employer and the servant must each have one, while a third copy will be required in all cases where an official has certified the making; countries using the individual contract mostly appear to find these sufficient. Where, however, the collective contract is still retained, additional copies will be necessary both in the district of recruitment and in that of employment if any attempt is to be made to trace the movements of single members of gangs. The tendency would seem to be towards the reduction of the numbers of copies required by means of the introduction of the individual contract in the form of a small book or permanent record retained by the employee.

Compulsion to resort to the contract appears in certain instances, in some cases for the benefit of the employer, in others in the interests of the native. Early Cape legislation introduced the compulsory contract in conjunction with Pass Laws, apparently with the object of regulating the movements of the native population; French law on the point varies, but renders the contract obligatory in many instances for the protection of the worker. The exemption of contracts in the case of engagements for less than one month seems to have originated in South Africa; it has since become fairly general. Most countries now maintain a permissive contract, allowing the employer to dispense with one if he finds himself able to do so, the presumption being that the native's interests will be protected in such cases by the probability that only the best and most popular employers will be able to maintain their labour supply without this precaution.

The length of the contract also varies greatly, though in almost every code there is some limitation. Early South African law put the limit at five years; modern legislation has steadily decreased this term. The Belgian Congo makes the period three years, as do the Portuguese colonies; French law limits it to two years, the figure adopted by the British East African group, though Tanganyika again limits this to one year by Governor's proclamation, while Swaziland admits only 360 working days. Generally, there would appear to be a steady trend of opinion towards the shorter periods.

The question is a difficult one, with very conflicting elements. On the one hand, the long contract favours reduction of costs of recruiting and carriage, it lessens recruiting fees, it tends to produce a more experienced and skilful worker, it makes for reliability in the supply of labour, and it impels the employer to do his best for his servants in order to encourage them to undertake the long contract.

Against this there can be very little doubt that the prolonged absence of a number of men from home is deleterious to the general welfare of the native community, whether they have left on contract or gone to seek work independently. All available evidence from various countries on the desirability or otherwise of the wage-earning habit tends to emphasize the fact that the evils increase rapidly with the longer periods of absence; the Belgian Commission on Labour in the Congo stressed this point, while the worst results of absence are reported from Nyasaland, where men are away for several years at a time, although the contract is rare.

The matter would seem to be one requiring most careful consideration by governments if they are to safeguard adequately the welfare of the native population as a whole as against the interests of the employer, and to some extent those of the worker.

The utility and maintenance of the contract are closely bound up with the question of the identification of the traveller, a subject which must be dealt with separately.

XII. THE VALUE OF THE CONTRACT

THE advantages and disadvantages of the contract to all concerned now require consideration, for there is at present a general lack of agreement in the attitude of governments; some appear to tolerate it only with suspicion, while others consider it worthy of legal enforcement.

The crux of the matter is undoubtedly the nature of the contract; the old form, in which it was little more than a legal trap for the unwary native, can merit little support; the case is, however, very different where a genuine agreement for mutual benefit is contemplated.

From a governmental point of view, the contract has many conspicuous advantages. It admits of the compilation of statistics of the greatest importance in supervising the welfare of a native community, it keeps the administrator informed about the movements and activities of his people, it is a valuable aid to the doctor in his efforts to observe and combat endemic diseases, it enables headmen or relatives to be informed as to the whereabouts of absent friends, it facilitates the collection of taxes, it introduces control over the exodus in search of work, and generally it regularizes and clarifies a state of affairs that otherwise may lead to the growth of evils without detection.

For the recruiter it is indispensable. He cannot send a batch of men to an employer without any sort of stipulation about the period for which they are to work, nor can he make his advances or payments of taxes unless he has some legal claim to recovery; he will also need the support of an official in making his agreement with his recruits, to impress upon them the fact that they are undertaking definite obligations. Without a contract he cannot risk the expenditure involved in his business, nor can he ensure that his recruits will go to the client for whom he has obtained them, and not be tempted aside by specious offers from rivals, since crimping can only imply incitement to breach of contract between certain definite persons where such a contract exists.

The employer needs the contract, since he generally has to rely to a considerable extent on the recruiter, and without stipulated terms of service it is obviously impossible for the two to do business; he also requires some definite information regarding the probable future fluctuations of his labour supply. Again, he needs some protection against unscrupulous neighbours who may try to decoy away his employees, especially in case of seasonal shortage. The protection of the medical inspection of recruits is also dependent on the contract, and without this there is the possibility of having to deal with a batch of men who show an abnormal sick rate, with consequent trouble and expense. In any case of dispute, the written agreement enables the matter to be speedily settled, and eliminates sudden demands for advance in wages or other possible extortion. Also, when dealing with men who will remain for some considerable period, he is able to do more for their welfare, since he can spend on this the money otherwise sunk in additional recruiting, when the necessity for frequent replacements arises. In the case of any new enterprise, the contract is almost indispensable, since it will probably be necessary to go to some expense in bringing men from a considerable distance, and this can obviously not be incurred if there is to be no sort of hold over the recruits when they have arrived.

It is, however, the native worker who stands to benefit most from the contract. When leaving home, it enables him to obtain an advance of wages, or settle the question of his tax, and it secures him the benefit of the recruiter's arrangements for the journey, in the place of the arduous march with inadequate resources. It is usually supervised by a government official, who explains the conditions, pay, and nature of work to him, and ensures that the contract is in these particulars definite and precise; he is guaranteed certain benefits such as his return home, and a record is made which will enable him to be accounted for in case of death or misadventure, his wages due being collected and secured for his relatives. Also, he is medically examined, and thereby safe-guarded from attempting work for which he is physically unfit, while he may also thus have detected, and receive treatment for, some disease such as hookworm or yaws, which he had previously neglected. In case of any dispute with his employer he has a definite record of the original agreement, so that he can claim redress if required to accept work for which he did not originally offer himself, or otherwise agree to conditions inferior to those which he was led to expect. So manifest are the advantages of the honest contract to the worker, and so precarious is his position without one, that it is remarkable that the native is not more strongly in favour of it; nevertheless, both in the British East African group and in French West Africa, a considerable degree of hostility to the contract is reported. It seems probable, however, that this is attributable to the memory of the former type of contract that was little more than a trap, and also to the constant suspicion of the African when confronted by any sort of examination of his intentions or movements.

A matter which can only be regulated by the completion of a contract is the advance of wages; in the case of illiterate natives it is important that some written statement of any obligation of this nature should be drawn up at the time of incurring it. The great majority of workers, when leaving home, wish to make various arrangements which entail small payments, and for this purpose they require an advance of wages. This then becomes an attraction in recruiting, and an agent who refuses to make any such concession will speedily find himself outdistanced by his more accommodating rival; further, a cut-throat competition may well set in when competing recruiters give increasing advances, until a point is reached where men are offered a large proportion of the whole of the pay due for the contract.

The evils of such an arrangement are obvious; the sanction of considerable debts on the part of ignorant natives is in itself undesirable, while it may also lead to peonage when employed; in addition, it is clearly an incentive to the worker to break his contract and go to seek work with some employer to whom he is not heavily in debt. It is also eventually disastrous for the recruiter, who finds himself losing an increasing proportion of the money paid out in this form. The matter may thus usefully be included in the contract, when the exact amount can be specified, and supervision of this rendered possible to enforce any requisite limitation.

Most codes admit of some advance, but where allowed it is almost always limited; the figure selected naturally depends largely on the rate of wages contemplated. South Africa fixes the figure at five pounds; Basutoland puts it at two pounds. An interesting system of gradation is to be found in Tanganyika where the advance is limited to payment of the annual tax plus half a month's wages in order to meet the considerable differences in rates of pay which are to be found in that country.

In some parts there is also the 'bush' advance to be found; the native receives a sum previous to the completion of any contract, often several months earlier; he is then expected to come forward in due course and contract for work, acknowledging the receipt of the advance when doing so. This arrangement is a method of securing a lien on the services of the man before competing recruiters are in the field, so that a supply of labour can be kept in reserve, available for use when required. Under most laws, this is not legally recoverable, and either the honesty of the native or some form of illicit pressure is relied upon to secure acknowledgement of the obligation. This system is clearly objectionable, and it is far preferable for any advance to be made and recorded only at the date of contract.

The practice of giving advances in kind rather than in cash, with its extension in the form of presents to the women, is of course a species of truck and objectionable as such; most codes render it illegal as being payment of wages in kind.

The contract can also usefully be made to cover the case of wives or families who are accompanying their menfolk to work; conditions under which this is approved can be shown, all doubt as to maintenance or repatriation liabilities being thus cleared up.

The main feature of the contract is, however, one that is generally overlooked; its merits or demerits are considered from the point of view of the existing situation, and there is often a lack of appreciation of its most important function as a forerunner of collective bargaining, and a labour market in every way better regulated. In all parts of the world, the development of industrialism tends to produce combinations of the workers to defend their interests, while, on the other hand, the employers also agree on the terms which they are prepared to offer; however much these arrangements may interfere with the absolute liberty of the individual, they seem to be inevitable in practice, if only on account of the advantages derived by both sides from such methods of bargaining. In Africa, however, the labourer is hardly ever sufficiently advanced to be able to organize to this degree, and trade unions in the European form are still quite in their infancy even where they exist at all. The worker's interests are cared for by the various governments according as this is considered necessary, and such action as is taken by the native himself consists mainly of the boycotting of unpopular employment as far as this may be possible; elementary strikes and disturbances caused by specific grievances represent almost the only concerted action. Supply and demand alone regulate conditions (except where arbitrary wage-fixing machinery exists) and there is a constant danger of undue advantage being taken by one side or the other, in instances of acute shortage of workmen in the one case or distress among the native population in the other. Wages fluctuate irregularly, and the supply of labour is unreliable; each individual enterprise makes its own bargains, and the worker comes or goes as he feels inclined, or can be cajoled by plausible touts; the whole labour market is erratic and disorganized, and all concerned suffer accordingly.

When, however, resort to the contract becomes general, conditions are at once much more clearly defined; without any actual organization, the terms of employment in the various areas will tend to conform, and the native will learn to rely on his written contract as interpreted by a disinterested official; the more experienced will guard the interests of their ignorant brethren, and it will no longer be so likely that vague rumours of astonishing conditions, either good or bad, elsewhere will upset a whole community of labourers. A far closer watch over the fluctuations of the market can be maintained, and any alteration in conditions can be carried out after discussion, when the official can (under present conditions) represent the views of the workpeople, and the change can be introduced with general agreement. Any attempt at collective bargaining, wage-fixing, or other regulation of labour conditions as a whole must depend on the general acceptance of certain terms, and if rights are admitted for either side duties will also be entailed. Haphazard and disorganized bargaining between individuals must afford opportunity for profit to the cunning and unscrupulous, whether employer or servant; the clear definition of terms will safeguard the interests of the honest workman equally with those of the upright employer. Realization of the principle of the bargain is essential for the worker's progress; while he is in a strong position usually, owing to his power of the boycott, he is also much in need of protection in such matters as repatriation expenses, hospital treatment, compensation for injury or sickness, and other advantages, and until he holds a demonstrable agreement by which some employer is rendered liable for such assistance he is obviously open to exploitation by any unscrupulous person who wishes to shirk obligations. The native frequently fails to recognize this, and consequently avoids any contract, regarding it as being merely an irksome restriction of his own right to suit himself entirely as to how, when, and where he works. The attitude is comprehensible in the ignorant native, but progress will be impossible until both master and servant are able to work on a basis of mutually agreed rights and duties.

The compulsory resort to the contract is being tried in parts of Africa; the general tendency would appear to be rather in the direction of its voluntary use, with increasing reliance on it for the enforcement of welfare measures.

XIII. THE IDENTIFICATION OF THE WORKER

A DIFFICULTY which underlies many aspects of labour problems is the question of devising some means for ensuring the identification of the worker; the problem arises both in connexion with the requirements of the master and with any measures taken for the welfare of the servant.

The employer needs some means of ascertaining the identity of the man with whom he is dealing; he must know that one and the same individual is concerned in the original contract, its subsequent carrying out, and the observance of the mutual obligations involved; he must be assured that his workman is the one shown as having been medically examined previous to engagement, and he cannot be expected to undertake care in sickness, compensation for disablement, or repatriation expenses, unless he is sure that he is dealing with his genuine employee. In case of breach of contract, no steps can be taken unless it be possible first to establish the liability of the defendant, and advances of wages or payment of tax can only be made when there is some assurance that the beneficiary will make an adequate return.

The native on his side also needs some means of proving his identity. His claims to the benefits secured him, whether by law or by the terms of his contract, will be based on this; any complaint of breach of contract on the part of his employer must be preceded by proof that this employer is really liable, and in case of disaster while journeying between his home and his place of employment he is obviously advantageously placed if he can prove that he has certain contractual rights to assistance. Again, any system of deferred wages, remittance to relatives at home, or payment of tax while absent, will depend on the establishment of proof of identity, while in case of death the same necessity arises in connexion with forwarding property to heirs. It is also of great importance to him that he should be in a position to prove his origin when travelling, or he may be called upon to pay some tax or due which he has already satisfied at home, or some unscrupulous headman may require him to serve as a porter or carry out other communal obligations for which he is not legally liable.

From the point of view of the administration it is equally important that the identity of the workman should not be in doubt; without this assurance, medical precautions and quarantine rules must fall to the ground, and the worker himself will lose their protection, while a great risk will arise of the dissemination of disease. Tax records, also, cannot be accurately kept unless the payer is definitely known, while headmen or relatives will lose trace of their people if these cannot be identified elsewhere.

Unfortunately, the African is very casual in the use of names; tribal custom may provide him with several, while he also readily assumes a nickname; there is in addition the difficulty of correct spelling when recording. Some tribes, again, have a ceremonial objection to the use of the name of a father, or a person who has died, and this serves to introduce complications, especially for persons ignorant of the tribal custom, as all strangers will naturally be. There is in addition the widespread tendency of the native to regard a correct record with suspicion; he fears that some unknown and probably oppressive use may be made of any information about himself which he may supply, and he therefore frequently purposely gives false particulars; he may even adopt a vulgar or indecent pseudonym as an excellent joke in the vernacular for the amusement of his fellows who alone understand it.

This state of affairs renders it most difficult to establish identity by means of recorded names alone; even when the native himself is extremely anxious to prove his origin, he may be quite unable to do so, and may suffer considerable injustice in consequence. The difficulty has arisen in all parts of Africa, and has been dealt with in very varied ways.

The matter is, of course, far more than a problem connected only with labour; it is an important administrative question involving police measures, quarantine maintenance, taxation, and various other aspects of native life; the subject is one which presents many difficulties and which might be dealt with at great length; it is proposed to restrict the present examination to the effect upon the labourer.

Unfortunately, the wider problem is one which has aroused much heated controversy; in some cases legislation has introduced a measure of control over all movement that can only be regarded as oppressive, while in other instances the advocates of the entire liberty of the individual have successfully opposed the introduction of any method of identification whatever, to the undeniable detriment of the traveller in many cases.

Probably few Europeans realize the extent to which all modern society depends upon the establishment of identity; so entirely has this become a part of the ordinary life of the community that the working of the system passes unnoticed. But on it depends the exercise of all civic rights or functions; without it no legal claim can be sustained, no pension or compensation paid, no credit obtained or cheque cashed, no marriage celebrated nor death certificate granted, nor will any testimonial of character or competency be possible. To realize the importance of this factor, it is only necessary to imagine the plight of a traveller stranded in some distant European capital, where he is unknown to any one, and has lost all means of establishing his identity; he would certainly have a most unpleasant experience even if an educated man and a linguist. The simpler needs of the African render him less dependent on such machinery, but he, nevertheless, is liable to meet with many mishaps if he travel far from his home without any sort of record of his origin; that natives themselves feel this is borne out by their anxiety to secure some sort of paper or pass, preferably of an official nature, before setting out on a journey.

Methods of identification are apt to be regarded as synonymous with pass laws; this, however, is by no means the case; the two are closely connected and cannot be altogether separated, but measures should be considered from the point of view of their intention: are they meant for the benefit and protection of the individual, whether native or non-native, or are they rather constructed to facilitate control of vagabondage, detection of crime, or similar police activities?

Early legislation was mainly directed towards the regulation of the movements of natives, and, in the extreme cases, it was obviously intended to establish a wide measure of control in the interests of employers; the various laws of the Cape in the early and middle years of the nineteenth century were all directed towards ensuring an adequate supply of agricultural labourers, and took little account of the native point of view. Subsequent modifications were complicated by the differing legislation in the British Colonies and the Dutch Republics, and certain discrepancies still exist. The great increase of employment which followed mining development led to special laws to meet local needs, and the labour district system (see Part II, Union of South Africa) came into being, where special control was exercised, a complicated organization with a considerable staff to work it being necessitated. Generally the South African regulations remain principally pass laws, and are designed more to meet the needs of the mining industry with its peculiar conditions than those of agriculture.

In Kenya a registration system was introduced after the War, intended to suit an agricultural community; it also necessitated a considerable staff, for a young country, with elaborate arrangements for the recording of finger-prints; the cost, however, is generally considered to have been justified by results. This system has been widely criticized as being humiliating and inquisitorial; its supporters, however, claim that there is nothing in it which can be oppressive to the honest native, while, on the other hand, it serves him in giving him a ready means of establishing his identity, and in addition furnishes a valuable safeguard against the danger of increasing vagabondage in the towns.

In the French colonies the problem has been approached rather from the labour than from the police point of view; the provision of a book for the worker (*livret de travail* in Madagascar and Equatorial Africa, *livret d'identité* in West Africa) in which all relevant details are entered, and in which the terms of any engagement are recorded, would seem to form a sort of combined contract and certificate of identity. In the Belgian Congo trial has been made of the metal token system, where a taxpayer is given a numbered disk relating to the register on which he pays; this, of course, is easily connected with any contract if necessary. In the Portuguese colonies, some use is made of the tax ticket as a means of identification in connexion with labour.

The actual means of establishing proof is a matter of difficulty; it is much to be regretted that the use of finger-prints for this purpose first made its appearance in connexion with criminals, since this otherwise excellent method of identification has thus come to be regarded with aversion; without it the task of recognizing an illiterate person with certainty is vastly increased. Signatures not being available, photographs are almost the only alternative, and these must be costly and cumbrous in preparation to a degree that renders them almost useless. The increasing number of educated natives will no doubt in time lead to the use of their fairly recognizable signatures; meanwhile, the problem remains to complicate relations between master and servant, and create difficulties for both.

The whole question of identification has been dealt with in almost all of the African countries in some manner, with varying measures of success; it appears inevitable that increasing development and the growing complications thereby created will render some means of achieving the purpose essential in all countries. The matter is one which might well receive joint consideration from administrators on either side of international boundaries, since migration has a considerable bearing upon it.

XIV. PENAL SANCTIONS

THE question of the most satisfactory method of dealing with breach of contract and offences against labour laws is one which has arisen in every African country, and has given considerable trouble to administrators. The attempted solutions vary surprisingly, and it is clear that there is an entire lack of uniformity of practice or agreement on the principles involved.

The older laws were mainly intended to give legal support to the master's claim on his servant's services; breach of contract in the form of deserting from work or offences against an elaborate code could be punished with imprisonment or flogging in addition to fine; the employer was not included in the provisions, unless as being liable to fines in case of the infringement of certain elementary provisions for welfare. These old laws, in fact, reflect strongly the survival of slave-owner mentality; the early Masters and Native Servants Laws, indeed, were drawn up at a time when some rules were essential for the regulation of the freed slaves, and they naturally reproduce to a large extent the older standpoint.

Modern legislation, however, has tended to make the position more equitable; as welfare measures were included to protect the interests of the worker, so also were steps taken to make the other terms of the law accord better with civilized practice; the principle of the voluntary contract was upheld, and facilities were provided for enforcing observance of the terms by both parties, though the form of punishment usually differed for master and for servant.

In accordance with the trend of European legislation, the point has now been reached where the whole justifiability of penal sanctions in connexion with labour is disputed; the view is advanced that no such element should be included, but that such matters should be settled by civil action entirely, as in Europe. Even the most advanced codes in the colonies, however, fail to attain this standard, and the problem will be found on examination to present many difficulties.

An earlier section of the present investigation stressed the importance of the contract in improving relations between employer and worker; without definite and easily demonstrable terms of agreement, it will be impossible to prove the obligations on either side; no clear statement of conditions generally obtaining will be feasible, while welfare rules will fail in their purpose when no proof of liability for compliance is forthcoming. It thus becomes important that observance of the contract by both sides should be upheld, and the difficulty of achieving this is the outstanding cause of much labour trouble.

Adherence to terms of an agreement is a comparatively simple question in Europe, owing to the conditions existing there; the worker will in most cases be a member of a union or other body which will arrange the terms on which work is accepted, and subsequently any alteration or modification will be a matter of negotiation between the organizations on each side. Individually, the workman is usually very anxious to retain his job, since the supply of labour is probably far in excess of the demand; the whole welfare of himself and his family depends on his continued employment, and there is no doubt about his identity; he has some little property which he values, and he comes from a class that is well used to industrial conditions and to compliance with rules.

The African, however, is in an entirely different position, which is in most cases a far stronger one than that of the European worker. The lack of any union appears at first sight to be a severe handicap, and in certain parts some attempt to remedy this has been made; there are, however, other advantages which go far to compensate for any disability in that direction. Primarily, the African is very seldom in the position of being forced by economic pressure to work at any particular task; in most colonies the great bulk of the workers are still closely connected with the tribal lands and villages, from which they come and to which they will return; wives and families are provided for there, and the larger part of the wages earned will go to procure luxuries rather than necessities. Only in the Union of South Africa, to some extent in Katanga, and to a far lesser degree in some urban centres of the other countries, will any considerable population be found who are directly dependent on wages for their subsistence. This fact renders the worker singularly independent, and goes far to protect him against exploitation.

The second marked difference between European and African conditions lies in the fact that in the one unemployment is an

ever-present evil, while in the other there is in normal circumstances a constant shortage of labour, which may at times become
acute; this again greatly strengthens the position of the worker.

It thus follows that a system which works well in civilized circumstances breaks down seriously when applied to more primitive
conditions. To the European worker the threat of discharge is a
very grave one, menacing the standard of living for himself and his
family. To the African it means little; he merely returns home or
goes to another employer who is well pleased to secure his services;
in no way is his own comfort or that of his family appreciably
affected. Again, the European presumably possesses certain
chattels which make up his home, and these are liable to seizure
by civil procedure; the African's possessions (other than those
in his distant home) are usually limited to the clothes in which he
stands, and these, scanty though they may be, are largely superfluous. He is thus practically immune from punishment by civil
law, and he presents a real problem if any effort is to be made to
enforce the terms of some judgement against him.

Thus arises the need for some means of resorting to the criminal
law to reinforce the inadequate civil remedy, and some provision
of this nature will be found in every African code.

It may also be well to contrast the fate of the European worker
in trouble under civil law, and that of the African who has been dealt
with by the criminal code. The first may find that he is imprisoned,
not perhaps for debt but for disobedience to a magistrate's order;
he may be evicted from his home and see his property sold, and he
with his family may be reduced to subsistence on charity or some
small State allowance. The African may be sentenced to a short
term of imprisonment, not, under modern conditions, in most
colonies, usually a very unpleasant experience; he has no property
to lose, so does not suffer in that way, and his family are far away
and entirely unaffected by his vicissitudes. He has, of course, been
subjected to the disgrace of a criminal conviction, but this, since it
is a matter of the white man's opinion, leaves him quite unmoved.
It may thus well come about that the European worker is liable
to far greater hardship under civil law than the African under
criminal law.

It will be understood that the foregoing reflections are intended
to apply to the experience of the individual; they are not meant
to refer to the wider problem of the advisability of using the

machinery of the criminal law for purposes to which it may be ill adapted.

Examination of various codes will reveal penal clauses of some kind in all of them; the nature of these, however, varies, and this should be considered before criticism is directed at the formidable punishments which appear in some labour legislation. In Europe laws are complex and carefully designed for an exact purpose, the necessary machinery for their enforcement being available; in the colonies, however, far less elaborate arrangements must suffice, and it thus frequently occurs that one code has to cover the provisions of numerous different laws in civilized countries. So, while the legislation may be primarily intended to deal with labour matters, it will be found to include in its scope matters which in Europe would be dealt with by special laws, some civil and some criminal. A code which is intended to cover not only contract but employers' liability, workmen's compensation, factory acts, safety regulations, truck acts, sanitary rules, and a number of other subjects, must of necessity be wide in scope and inclusive in punishment. Most countries show a tendency to separate the various sections and to deal with each subject by special legislation; this, however, will be possible only with advanced conditions, for at a primitive stage it is important to avoid the compilation of a mass of laws requiring expert knowledge and ample machinery to administer them. Hence most existing codes will on examination prove to be omnibus laws, containing the germ of far more elaborate and detailed provisions which may be introduced at a later date when they prove desirable and workable.

Penal clauses may be divided into three classes: first, those intended for the maintenance of the terms of the contract; second, those enforcing regulations for safety or welfare; and third, punishments for acts likely to affect the community as a whole. It is obvious that the nature of the punishment for these various types of offence must admit of a severe sentence in serious cases; this explains the considerable terms of imprisonment which occur in certain codes.

A difference is sometimes made between major and minor offences, both on the part of the employer and that of the servant; generally, this will be found to classify these much in the terms of the preceding paragraph; in other words, minor offences are those which in more advanced communities are dealt with by civil procedure, while major offences are of the nature of breaches of factory acts, safety regulations, and similar laws.

There appears to be a general tendency towards the relegation of the lesser breaches of rules to what forms a kind of compromise between civil and criminal procedure; the employer or workman lays his complaint, and the case is dealt with by a special court, or a magistrate following special procedure; the method is a kind of compulsory arbitration, with the infliction of a fine as its result, and there is little suggestion of the criminal court about the hearing. The advantage lies in the fact that business can be dispatched more rapidly, while preliminary application to a lawyer is unnecessary; the machinery of the police-court is available in case of a refractory defendant, and the proceedings can be transformed into a criminal case if it appears during hearing that the offence is of a more serious nature.

This method for removing labour disputes from the atmosphere of the criminal courts is to be found in the *conseil d'arbitrage* of the French colonies, and this seems to be the most definite attempt at such a solution. In the British East African group, provision is made for special treatment of defendants, Tanganyika requiring the alternative of a fine in every minor case, before imprisonment is inflicted.

The weak point of this method lies in the difficulty which frequently arises in collecting any fine that may be imposed; while the employer can usually be made to pay, the labourer is often apparently devoid of any property on which a levy might be made; thus, unless the award of the court is to become farcical, resort to imprisonment is inevitable. It may, however, be claimed that such a result is not unlikely in the case of European procedure, where a recalcitrant debtor may find himself in prison for defying the order of a court.

Pending the introduction of separate legislation, it is obvious that severe penalties must be retained for such offences on the part of the employer as condoning or creating dangerous conditions, concealment of diseases, or other infringements involving risk to life or health; on that of the workman, adequate punishment must follow breach of safety regulations, misuse of fire or explosives, and, generally, acts likely to result in serious accidents or grave damage. Minor offences may to some extent be punished by withholding luxuries otherwise given as a bonus in addition to stipulated wages.

It would thus appear that penal sanctions and criminal procedure in dealing with offences connected solely with the relations between master and servant tend to be eliminated; a species of intermediate court seems likely to be created, to deal with contractual obligations, the heavier penalties being retained only for offences which would be severely treated in any country. The separation of the various sections of the law, and the distinction between the requirements of the contract and the safety or welfare measures, is no doubt desirable in the interests of clarity and regularity; on the other hand, it should be remembered that labour laws are likely to be administered in most cases by magistrates who are not professional lawyers, working in conditions where speed and simplicity are of importance to all concerned; the advantage of a general code covering all aspects of labour problems would, therefore, seem to justify its retention until a country has reached a decidedly advanced stage.

The actual form to be taken by the punishment also presents some difficulty; the means to hand consist of fine, imprisonment, and flogging, with some minor disabilities in certain cases. Modern opinion is increasingly opposed to the use of corporal punishment, at any rate in any but certain special classes of offence, and its use in conjunction with actual labour offences is growing rarer. At the same time, there is the problem of the best method of dealing with a delinquent who deserves an exemplary lesson, but who cannot be considered a positive criminal. Cases such as dangerous acts of mischief in connexion with fire, explosives, or machinery, or repeated disobedience of vital safety regulations, are the type of offence with which it is often difficult to deal; the culprit must be given a drastic deterrent, in the interests of himself and his fellows, and as a warning to others; yet he is probably not at all the type that should be imprisoned with actual criminals. Flogging is thus often advocated for such cases, though its retention is disappearing; the Italian code in Eritrea admits of the infliction of fifty lashes, while the South African law also allows caning of juveniles. The British East African group retain corporal punishment with a cane in the case of juveniles, apparently as an attempt to dispense with the imprisonment of young persons, in communities where reformatories or similar establishments are scarce: there is, however, a general tendency to abandon corporal punishment. Imprisonment, again, is undesirable even for more serious offences, if it entails mingling with hardened criminals, and for this reason certain countries have introduced a special class of jail for minor offences, where prisoners are separated from those convicted on grave charges. In circumstances where the social stigma of a term in prison is practically non-existent, as in Africa, the effect of a spell of confinement will be different from that in the case of a European; a deterrent and reformative result must be aimed at, while the serious risk of manufacturing professional criminals and recidivists must be guarded against. The fatal facility with which the African adapts himself to his social surroundings renders him specially liable to fall a prey to contaminating influences; he lacks the power to discriminate between minor offences and real crimes, and thus sees no difference between his own case and that of a really dangerous offender; he has come into collision with the European's law, but regards this as a misfortune rather than any sort of disgrace, and he may thus very readily become a regular 'jail-bird'. It seems probable that increasing resort will be had to the separation of the two types of prisoner, and that the reformatory will be more widely used in place of the jail, in accordance with the modified judicial procedure in dealing with the case.

The problem is only one aspect of the whole question of crime and punishment in Africa, which itself is beginning to receive increasing and much-needed study.

XV. THE WORKMAN AND THE LAW

SOME attention has been given to modern legislation and its provisions to safeguard the interests of the workman in health, safety, and contract rights, while at work; it may now be valuable to examine the extent to which the various African countries have reproduced such European measures as Workmen's Compensation, Employers' Liability, Factory Acts, Unemployment Insurance, and similar modern innovations.

At first sight it may appear that little has been attempted in such directions, and that the African is left far behind the employee of other countries in these matters. Closer examination will show, however, that a decided advance has been made in certain particulars, while the peculiarities of the position render other measures superfluous or unfeasible at present.

Firstly, Unemployment Insurance may be ruled out for the greater part of Africa, as being quite redundant; in all except parts of the Union of South Africa and in West Africa there is normally a shortage of labour to a greater or less degree, and it is most unlikely that any man will suffer any real hardship through inability to find employment. In addition, even in exceptional times when reduced numbers are required, the superfluous men will be able to return to their homes and find occupation and support there; only in the case of the natives who are entirely divorced from the land will any difficulty arise. Throughout the tropics, again, nature is so bountiful and the actual necessities of life are so simple and so easily procured that hardship is rare. (The close and essential connexion between the workman and the land will be discussed in a subsequent section.) Such being the case, it is obviously unnecessary to introduce any measures calculated to combat the evils of unemployment; only with the growth of large urbanized or industrialized areas will such problems make their appearance, and such development will in any case presumably receive adequate attention and control from the local administration with a view to minimizing the evils which may result; meanwhile, measures to deal with unemployment can be regarded as superfluous in most of the African countries.

Employers' Liability will be found embodied in a primitive form in most codes, usually combined with measures to provide Workmen's Compensation; safety measures are enforced and healthy conditions of living are required; accidents receive compensation and hospital treatment is provided for. Generally, mining regulations are the most stringent, and they will usually be found to require a much higher standard than that applicable to agriculture. This is of course only to be expected, in view of the greater risk and the less healthy conditions of mining as compared with field work, in addition to which the ample means and elaborate organization of the important mineral concerns render it far easier for welfare measures to be introduced.

A considerable difference will be found between accident compensation and that for disease; while the first exists in some form in all codes, the second is seldom provided for; exceptions exist in the case of the South African arrangements for dealing with miners' phthisis, while other mining laws have rudimentary provisions of similar intention.

There is for practical purposes a great difference between the two classes of compensation, and whereas the payment is usually a simple matter in the case of an accident, compensation for occupational disease introduces numerous complications.

In a European industrial community, health may be regarded as usually normal; there is no question of exceptional climate or different groups of workers with varying powers of resistance, nor should respectable conditions of work expose employees to any abnormal strain. In Africa, however, many novel factors make their appearance. It will be necessary to discriminate between the man who came to work already infected with malaria and the one who contracted it while employed; the new-comer may be seriously upset by conditions which are perfectly healthy for the old hand; certain tribes will flourish where others show an alarming sick-rate; while the carelessness of the African, combined with his reluctance to undergo treatment and his love for probably deleterious native remedies, all serve to complicate the position.

Again, medical staff on a scale and of an efficiency usually quite unattainable in Africa will be essential for any action for disease compensation. It is a simple matter to settle a case concerning loss of a leg or an arm, but the nature and origin of an illness must be questions quite beyond the ability of a magistrate to decide.

Thus this form of compensation is seldom attempted; the lack of it is to some extent remedied by the maintenance of adequate medical resources by the employer, and by State provision of free hospital and prophylactic treatment as far as funds allow of this; there appears to be little possibility of advancing further, except as conditions admit of more complicated measures.

With regard to accident compensation, a curious position arises in connexion with insurance against such risks; the general lack of companies to undertake such work renders the obligation unavoidable for the employer, and this is usually regarded as a misfortune; it is urged that the law should insist upon the liability being assumed by a large and reliable society, rather than permit it to rest with a possibly bankrupt employer, and the introduction of insurance companies is therefore strongly advocated. The difficult nature of such business in itself presents a formidable obstacle, but there is in addition a distinct disadvantage in such procedure.

An analysis of the cause of accidents among agricultural workers will show that the great majority are due to the carelessness or culpability of the victim; strict regulations regarding the use and control of machinery will be entirely disregarded, safety devices will be removed as merely hampering work, and fire or explosives will be used with utter disregard of safety; curiosity or recklessness will account for a large number of entirely avoidable accidents. Now such cases, if referred to an insurance company, would be contested in court, often with success, when the victim would receive nothing; the employer merely refers him to the company, who quote the decision of the magistrate, and the matter is at an end. If, however, there is no company on which to lay the responsibility, the employer himself must give or refuse payment, and in that case it will be found that very frequently the good name of the estate will be so much concerned that payment will be made even in cases where it would not have been supported by law; the amount is small, and it is wiser to pay this rather than contest it, in order to satisfy the victim and his friends.

Method of payment also presents real difficulty; a lump sum will be uselessly dissipated, while the ready remedy of a pension is inapplicable in the case of a man domiciled in some remote part where machinery for payment is scarcely existent; weekly grants which may entail a journey on foot of several days are obviously impossible, particularly if the payee is a cripple; monthly payments will be squandered; impersonation is a standing risk; and the administrative staff will probably be quite inadequate to deal with the extra business involved in an area where such pensioners may become numerous. Probably the most satisfactory method is the payment of a lump sum which can be invested for the benefit of the victim by some impartial authority; if a herd of cattle or goats can be secured, the natural increase will go far towards forming adequate provision; settlement will present much greater difficulties in an agricultural community, in which private ownership of land is probably not recognized.

Again, the fixing of the amount to be paid is another source of difficulty; a sum which will represent ample provision for a pastoralist from a remote village where prices are low will be quite inadequate for the town-dweller living in much more expensive surroundings; the introduction of the scale of definite sums payable for various injuries which is to be found in some codes is thus doubtfully satisfactory; it would seem preferable to leave the matter largely to the discretion of the court making the award.

The whole question of compensation with its various aspects presents a most difficult problem to the African administrator; circumstances as at present existing in most colonies render any satisfactory solution impossible; it appears inevitable that considerable progress in social development and organization will be necessary before this matter can be dealt with at all adequately.

Factory Acts have not so far assumed much importance, mainly owing to the absence of conditions necessitating them; Africa has in the main so far produced raw material, and the erection of machinery and buildings for the production of manufactured articles is at present restricted to a few advanced areas in South Africa. It is of course true that a considerable amount of preliminary work is necessary in connexion with exports before they are fit for sale, and this requires some factory equipment; ore must be reduced to ingots, cotton and sisal rendered fit for the market, coffee prepared, or sugar-cane crushed. These needs, however, produce in most cases only one group of buildings in the centre of the area which they serve; the work is part of the general production, and the employees live under the same conditions as the rest of the labour force. There is thus little likelihood of the creation of conditions similar in anyway to those of the great industrial centres of Europe, and such factories as do exist will be distributed over the country rather than grouped in urban conditions.

The circumstances of work, again, tend to the absence of many objectionable conditions likely to arise in temperate climates; a high temperature will necessitate free ventilation, reliable weather will enable much work to be done in the open air, while a tropical sun will eliminate any fear of unduly dark premises. Thus problems of floor space and cubic capacity as compared with numbers of workers hardly require consideration, and the risk of the creation of a deleterious dust-laden atmosphere is negligible. With the exception of certain processes connected with mining, for which provision is made, dangerous trades are virtually non-existent, and the nature of most of the African products is such that their preparation is unlikely to lead to the evolution of noxious gases or liquids.

The regulation of hours of work, again, is also largely affected by the conditions obtaining; night work in Europe is generally regarded as undesirable for many reasons, and restrictions are applied in the case of women and children; in the tropics, however, it may well prove preferable to work during the hours of darkness rather than in the heat of the day. Therefore, if adequate relays of workers are utilized, there seems to be little objection to continuous running of factories.

Most codes limit the hours of employment, but it is doubtful if this is very important; the usual standard is low, and the African promptly absents himself if he considers his task or hours unduly arduous, so that only a very exceptional keenness on the part of the employee is likely to furnish an example of overwork. Again, the independent status of the African worker will render acts of oppression by foremen or overseers almost impossible.

XVI. LIVING CONDITIONS AND THEIR EFFECT

IT is obviously in the interests of all concerned that the conditions in which the worker lives should be as far as possible healthy and agreeable; the employer wishes to reduce his sickness percentage and to maintain the popularity of his estate, while the Government in its capacity of guardian will exact certain minimum requirements. The combined incentives will produce conditions which are almost always an improvement on those obtaining in the home villages, while in the case of many large and wealthy organizations the accommodation and treatment of the workers can be regarded as of real benefit to them.

There is, however, a general tendency to regard such matters purely from the standpoint of the labourer; this is of course natural in the case of the employer, but for those concerned with the welfare of the native community as a whole it is important to consider the effect of the experience of the wage-earner upon his social *milieu*. The annual exodus and return of a considerable proportion of the adults of a community in search of work must have an important bearing on the well-being of the whole, and the results may be beneficial or disastrous with cumulative effect. The careful observation of these, with a view to the early control of objectionable tendencies, is the clear duty of an administration genuinely seeking the prosperity of its natives. It may therefore be useful to examine the results which may be expected to accrue from the acquirement of the wage-seeking habit.

Modern scientific research has emphasized the great importance of diet, not only in relation to the health of the individual but also as a factor in the welfare of a people; a well-balanced food-supply has indeed been proved essential for the maintenance of a race at its best in health, physique, and fertility. The discovery of the part played by the vitamins at all stages of life has thrown new light on problems of population, and increasing attention is being given to various dietaries and their effects.

Civilization in Europe has enabled enormous progress to be made in the food-supply; by means of acclimatizing exotic plants, extending the range of imports, and improving methods of preservation, the white man has been able to introduce a variety and adequacy into his diet scale that must soon go far towards abolishing deficiency disease in communities able to avail themselves of it fully. Other races remain more restricted in foodstuffs, and nowhere is this so conspicuous as in Africa.

In that continent conditions vary considerably; it is possible to find areas where the inhabitants are quite adequately nourished, as in large parts of the Union of South Africa; elsewhere, however, tribes can be found who live for most of the year on the borderline of disaster, and who, even though they may not be actually hungry, yet lack essential elements in their diet.

Over a large part of tropical and semi-tropical Africa, the tsetse fly restricts animal husbandry, and meat and milk are thus scarce; in considerable areas of the eastern countries and the Congo, the people regard any meat as a rare luxury, milk being even more scarce; thus the whole range of animal fats, with their vitally important constituents, is ruled out for those tribes. Instead, vegetable products must be used, while occasionally fish may be available in sufficiently large quantities to remedy the defect; such people will also generally be found to be almost omnivorous, so that insects, vermin, and various uninviting plants are included in the dietary in the effort to secure the missing elements. Nevertheless, the lack of such important constituents must have a serious influence on the tribes concerned. Another conspicuous deficiency is the general neglect of eggs as food; while chickens are to be found most widely distributed, they are rarely used for eating among the more primitive people, while eggs are almost universally considered to be suitable only for sale; some tribes, indeed, rank them as definitely unclean, and inflict penalties on the consumer of them. Thus another important source of valuable constituents is not available.

The inclusion of some anti-scorbutic in any diet is such an elementary necessity that the African has discovered this for himself; every tribe will be found to have some system of utilizing to the full such supplies of the requisite ingredient as are to be had. The native knowledge of wild spinach and edible grasses is wide, while he is quick to take advantage of novelties such as new fruits or vegetables, once he has experimented with them. The wet season and the months following it will admit of the consumption of considerable quantities of green food, while the method of brewing the various beers as a rule also ensures an important addition to the anti-scorbutic element; occasionally, where the supply is at all times of year somewhat meagre or where the dry season is of long continuance, it will be found that means of drying the green vegetables have been discovered, so as to admit of their preservation throughout the period of scarcity; it is interesting to observe that the method is one which preserves the delicate vitamin content with considerable success.

Fruit is restricted in variety and limited in season in the average village; bananas are widespread and of great value, while in certain areas coco-nuts are important not only as an addition to diet, but also for their many subsidiary uses. The mango is commonly found, and other fruit-trees such as limes, custard apple, guavas, oranges, pine-apples and similar exotic plants, occur where alien influence has led to their introduction; these, however, are seldom to be found in the more primitive parts, and they are in any case in season only for a short while, storage not being practised.

Sugar seldom enters into the native dietary except in the form of the cane, eaten in its natural state, or made into a drink; the purchase of the prepared article comes only with experience of Europeanized conditions, though it is readily adopted especially as an addition to tea or coffee.

Preserved, tinned, or dried foods scarcely occur in the food of the ordinary native, for whom they are usually far too expensive, while in addition they are generally regarded with considerable suspicion. If, however, they are once introduced, they prove very popular; it seems probable that a valuable trade in such products might be cultivated, as the African begins to seek further variety in his food.

The normal dietary of the village is thus restricted to a large proportion of grain, or alternatively, yams, sweet potatoes, or cassava, with a varying but almost always scanty addition of meat in some form; green food and fruit, also honey, make a seasonal appearance, but are generally lacking for a great part of the year. Milk, butter, cheese, and eggs are almost unknown to very many natives, while fish is a rarity except in favoured regions.

To make matters worse, many tribes maintain a ban on various valuable local products, and game, fish, eggs, or other useful adjuncts may be debarred from the dietary through prejudice; while this tends to disappear when in contact with strangers, it is a potent force in the more primitive communities and has a most unfortunate influence in restricting the already scanty choice.

The dangerous limitations of such a diet are obvious, and the lack of essential constituents must make itself felt to a serious degree; the African's standard is repletion, and he therefore considers himself well fed as long as hunger is satisfied; thus, serious undernourishment may exist in a community which is quite content with the available supplies. (In this connexion the Kenya medical service has carried out some very interesting research into the diets of the Kikuyu and Masai.)

The acquirement of the work-seeking habit emphasizes this state of affairs, and brings to light many troubles which result from ill-balanced diet; the delicate equilibrium of health may not be disturbed as long as only the conditions in the village have to be resisted, and a community may seem healthy enough to the casual observer; if, however, recruiting is permitted, it is highly probable that the change combined with the effort to perform unaccustomed work will serve to bring out various ailments, possibly in a serious form. Thus, scurvy is a constant threat, beriberi, xerophthalmia, and other deficiency diseases being also liable to occur; in addition, dysentery and digestive troubles frequently result from the change of diet, even though this may be for the better.

So general is this condition that many employers have adopted the system of retaining new recruits in special camps under observation and with a light régime of work; food may be adapted to their needs, and careful medical attention is paid to their condition. It is found that this greatly diminishes sickness, and the cost is thus economically justified.

In these cases, however, the circumstances only come to light in a practical way in connexion with the efficiency of the worker; no corresponding action is taken in the case of the rest of the tribe who remain at home, though their condition is presumably similar. It thus appears probable that many tribes are for an appreciable part of each year definitely undernourished, though neither they nor the casual observer may be aware of this fact.

That the African is in many cases conscious of the situation is shown by the number of work-seekers who will give food shortage as their reason for leaving home, in which case there is definite insufficiency, and not only a lack of certain constituents. But the startling avidity with which citrus fruit and other anti-scorbutics will be consumed by travellers shows that there is a very definite natural craving for these elements, even though the men may appear well enough nourished. The need for other vitamins may be equally great, even if less conspicuous.

The importance of this sinister state of affairs will be obvious; research seems to demonstrate increasingly the dominant part played by food in building up resistance to disease and maintaining the physical functions in full vigour. Probably the expectant and the nursing mothers suffer most from the lack of the necessary constituents in their diet, and it seems likely that the high infant mortality characteristic of so many tribes is attributable in some measure to food limitations. Adolescents must also be affected, and normal full development will be impossible for a child who is for recurrent periods deprived of certain essential elements.

In the case of a tribe living in such conditions, the absence of a proportion of its adults at work must have a very distinct effect; they will mostly be youths and young men, the future fathers of families, and if they can be provided with a varied and generous diet containing the elements lacking in their homes, their health, and that of the next generation, will benefit to that extent. Also, their absence will leave a larger share of the available food constituents to be consumed by those remaining at home, thus improving conditions in the village. Again, the experience acquired while at work will encourage the returning labourer to extend the scope of his dietary both by disregarding old prejudices and by utilizing novel kinds of food. Repatriated recruits will often be found to be carrying seeds of some plant which they consider likely to be an asset in their homes, and the African seems to be fully alive to such possibilities; arrangements for encouraging and facilitating this development should therefore meet with ready success.

It is common to hear that recruits have greatly improved in physique and health while at work, and the reports of prison departments usually show the same effect of a generous diet; so far, however, there appears to be little material available to show how the general physical condition of a tribe may have been affected by the habitual seasonal absence of a proportion of its adults at work.

Less important than diet perhaps, but nevertheless of considerable influence, must be the experience of improved conditions of accommodation. Modern labour lines are almost always superior in construction to the native type of house, while of necessity due attention will be paid to sanitation as a safeguard against outbreaks of disease among the workers. All up-to-date concerns provide facilities for bathing and washing of clothes, while more or less well-constructed and maintained latrines will introduce the raw native to the idea of special provision of this nature, too often a conspicuous shortcoming in the home village. He will also meet with rules for the safeguarding of the drinking-water supply, and will learn something of the evils of contaminating this.

Such conditions will do much to benefit the health of the labourers, and in the case of a well-conducted concern should go far to help in the elimination of hookworm and similar diseases; weatherproof houses and medical attention will reduce lung trouble, while various parasitic diseases and skin affections will receive attention. The returning labourer should thus be definitely improved in all such matters, and therefore in decidedly better health on his arrival in the village; in addition, however, he will have experienced the advantages of cleanliness and will view with more critical eyes the very primitive arrangements with which he was formerly satisfied. He cannot of course reproduce the permanent buildings in which he has been housed, but he will probably be somewhat more particular about his water-supply and the cleanliness of his surroundings. African apathy may extinguish individual effort, but there will at any rate be created a mentality more favourable to the activities of reforming authority.

In the matter of clothes alone, improvement is unfortunately unlikely. The labourer will usually favour the cheapest articles, and these will be either flimsy cotton garments or imported second-hand heavy clothing that speedily becomes insanitary and does not admit of adequate washing. In place therefore of the scanty dress of skins that his fathers wore, he will adopt cotton shorts and trousers, with perhaps a thick overcoat of doubtful origin; these will be worn continuously, whether wet or dry, and must prove a fertile source of chills and colds, while also spreading infection of all kinds. The provision, and the encouragement of the sale, of suitable healthy articles of clothing should therefore be pressed in the interests of the native.

In minor ways the returning worker will introduce a different mental attitude; a greater use of imported tools and utensils will occur, while some sort of illuminant at night will be appreciated; reading may not have been learnt, but the performances of literate acquaintances will have been observed, the already keen African respect for education being thus stimulated.

The effects of wage-seeking upon the village community are numerous and diverse; the subject is one which may well receive careful attention from the administrator.

XVII. MORAL EFFECTS OF WAGE-EARNING

IN the last chapter an attempt was made to review the physical results produced on the native community by the absence of a proportion of its male members at work at a distance; it will now be apposite to consider the moral effect of the position.

Unfortunately, from this point of view, the influence of the wage-earning habit is by no means as generally beneficial as it is physically; while employment under good conditions should prove to be of real advantage as far as health is concerned, there are many dangers connected with it from an ethical standpoint, and the welfare of the community may be gravely affected thereby.

Considering first the case of the worker himself, it is clear that he is exposed to numerous influences which will be entirely strange to him, from the moment that he leaves his village. The journey to work will itself be a novel experience for one accustomed to consider it unsafe to venture far from home, away from the protection of tribal law, among other tribes for whom the life of a stranger has little sanctity. Normal life must be to a great extent interrupted, and the tribal authorities satisfied about all social obligations before they will acquiesce in the venture; the complicated system of family loans and obligations in which the African lives must be dealt with to guard against distraint or other action during the worker's absence elsewhere; the family must be provided for, and some one must be found to act as guardian of home interests. If the journey is a long one, there will be the alarming possibilities of robbery, attack, or illness on the way, against which the only insurance is the solidarity of the party setting out.

On arrival at the place of employment, the recruit will have to face a formidable array of regulations and formalities; he will probably have been medically examined before, but this may be repeated. He will then be allotted quarters in the labour lines, where he and his friends form a tiny unit in the crowd of natives of other tribes. The routine of the life must be learnt, and a measure of discipline and method acquired by a man who has never previously had to trouble himself about time or date. Strange food will be issued to him, very likely of a kind that will disagree with him at first, while cooking in a method that will ensure the observance of tribal requirements is probably impossible. Various other infringements of tradition are inevitable, and the novice lives in a state of anxiety about the result, until he loses faith in the ancestral beliefs. Female society will be limited and undesirable, while the new-comer must make acquaintance with a standard of life in sexual matters which is entirely opposed to normal Bantu views. Opportunities will be ample for the purchase of all sorts of striking novelties, mostly useless and some pernicious; second-hand clothes of quite unsuitable European type will replace healthy nudity, and an occasional chance may occur to acquire a taste for the black man's outstanding peril, European liquor. Housing is probably of a type quite unlike any native dwelling, while illness or disease leads to detention in a sinister building where the patient is separated from his friends and made to submit to a strange diet and treatment, while the knowledge that the white doctors are addicted to cutting up people both dead and alive forms a persistent nightmare.

Some occurrence may render him unclean or bring him under other tribal ban, removable only under the auspices of the qualified native authority; the latter will of course not be available, so the burden must be borne or resort must be had to some unorthodox local practitioner. The victim, however, soon learns that the dire effects which he has always believed would follow any infringement of tribal law do not in practice occur, so he grows to despise them and the elders who have in the past interpreted them for him.

African adaptability will probably enable him to settle down in the new surroundings without too much discomfort, and intercourse with strangers will give him a broader outlook; things which shocked him on first arrival will soon become familiar and normal. The community spirit which so largely dominates the African's behaviour will have been broken down by contact with the wider world, and the old rules for guidance will no longer receive respect.

Such an experience must greatly change the worker, and he will return to his village home with a very different outlook; he has acquired an attitude of scepticism towards ritual observances, and has perforce braved the spiritual terrors held over the heads of infringers of tribal custom. His respect for the elders of the community will have been greatly weakened, and he is likely to

become a social rebel disliked and suspected by the more conservative and steadier element of society.

Accident may bring him into conflict with tribal law; he may
find his hard-earned wages impounded to pay his share of a family
fine, when his loyalty to the established system will be severely
strained. His property or family may have suffered during his
absence, and his appeal to the village heads will be prejudiced by
their dislike of his subversive opinions; his wife may be in the
house of another man, and his efforts at redress may meet only with
the reply that he should not have been away for so long.

There is also the possibility that he may have returned infected
with venereal disease, with obviously disastrous effects on his
family life.

It is not suggested that these results are likely to occur in every
case, or that they cannot be largely reduced; they are, however,
summarized as an indication of the disturbing nature of the forces
to which the novice is likely to be exposed.

The effect in the villages will be equally pronounced. A
primitive and self-contained community will be exposed to an
influx of returning travellers who have experienced entirely novel
methods of life; new ideas will be imported, and old observances
and codes will be criticized; tribal law and authority, formerly
unquestioned, will be disputed or ignored.

It cannot be expected that the elders, accustomed to be regarded
as the exponents of the ancient and infallible rules, will not resent
such an attitude; the subversive element will be regarded with
extreme hostility, as being disruptive of all moral standards, and
the offenders will be subjected to marked disapproval. The fact
that tribal law derives its authority so largely from the support of
supernatural penalties for infringement renders it very vulnerable
to the attacks of the sceptic, and the community is thus divided
into two hostile elements with irreconcilable views. The elders
will be alarmed and shocked at the result produced by foreign
adventure on their young men, and will accordingly become steady
and determined opponents of the wage-seeking habit.

The position of the women will also be affected, for, apart from
the possibility of actual infection, disputes are sure to arise as a
result of the long absence of the husbands, while the laxer morals
of the returned workers will tend to corrupt their families; a life of
prostitution, virtually unknown to primitive Bantu society, will

become a possibility. According to European ideas, the standard of many primitive tribes is low; there is, however, reason for believing that they regard paid prostitution as something entirely alien and shameful, and that a woman attempting to live such a life in the uncontaminated African community would receive very summary treatment. Once, however, the laxer attitude of the labour compound is introduced, either by the men or by wives who have accompanied their husbands to work, there is a general tendency for the old standard to be broken down, and genuine marriage is replaced by a temporary union that may lack even a nominal sanction. Where Islam is influential, the easy divorce permitted by it will prove far more attractive than the observance of the old Bantu family obligations in such transactions.

In any case, it is obvious that the herding together of large numbers of men with but little female society must produce undesirable results, and unnatural practices are a constant menace.

The greater contentment and better health of the married worker are so generally recognized that many employers are to be found who will go far in concessions for the benefit of the man who wishes to come accompanied by his wife; travelling expenses are paid, additional rations are issued, and special housing accommodation is provided, in varying degrees, and in some instances an appreciable proportion of the workers will be found to have their wives with them. In such cases, these will of course be greatly benefited, and the potential evils of the compound will be largely reduced.

The employer will naturally aim at retaining such people on his property; the longer the husband remains, the better his knowledge of his work, and the less the proportionate cost of bringing the family there in the first instance; so every encouragement is given to such cases to remain on. Here, however, the tribal influence is in opposition; the party will naturally tend to become homesick after a time, while there will also be anxiety about interests left behind, so that sooner or later the family will be found on their return journey. They may perhaps have had enough of alien adventure, and may drop back into village life permanently, or they may stay for a while and then feel a call for the more entertaining life of the wage-earner. Occasionally they will settle permanently on the place of employment, and cut themselves adrift finally from tribal life.

This last type will be found chiefly among the more skilled and higher-paid employees of the large companies, or as 'squatters' on farms, or, again, as doubtfully desirable additions to a floating urban population; wherever they are, they present a difficult problem to the administrator. Divorced from the old tribal traditions and restraints, they no longer have a mass of public opinion to guide and control their actions; it is unlikely that they will have become genuine converts to some other faith, though very possibly they are nominal Christians or Mahometans. For practical purposes, however, they are without any real standard of behaviour, and obey only such police or company regulations as may be effectively enforced. The ease with which such people may drift into the criminal classes, or the fertile ground which they will provide for inflammatory political propaganda, must be obvious.

In the villages, such developments are quite realized by the elders, in so far as they recognize the possibility that a man who leaves accompanied by his wife may never return; their traditional anxiety to preserve and extend the tribe therefore renders them hostile to the departure of that woman, and it will generally be found that the native authorities are openly or secretly exerting their influence to discourage this, even when they may be quite favourable to the exodus of the men who may be expected to bring back additional wealth to the village. Congestion in native reserves will of course reverse this attitude and act as an incentive to migration.

It is possible that the usual attitude of the tribal authorities towards the departure of women with their husbands is not really so well advised, even from their point of view, as they imagine. The presumption is that the work-seeker who has left his family behind him will feel this as a tie, and may thus be relied upon to return eventually. In practice, however, it may well occur that he forms a union with a woman of the neighbourhood in which he is employed, who is naturally strongly opposed to joining another tribe of which she knows nothing, and the man has thus an incentive to remain away permanently. If, however, he has been accompanied by his tribal wife, the couple will retain old habits and associations to a greater degree, and a return to their original home is far likelier. It would thus seem that the practice of wives accompanying their husbands tends to ensure the return of a greater proportion of the men, even though in a few cases the couple may be permanently lost to the tribe. There is thus considerable difficulty in the way of the realization of the object of some companies—the establishment of a small community of workers accompanied by their families, and living under much the same social conditions as those of the uncontaminated tribe. While this may in itself be probably the most salutary solution of the problem, it must involve the steady depletion of the home population, and will therefore meet with strong opposition from those interested in the welfare of the tribe. So a definite conflict arises between the interests of the migrant worker and those of the village community which he is leaving; inevitable progress and the consequent displacement of population seem likely to perpetuate this divergence, and the satisfactory settlement of the difficulty presents one of the greatest of the problems connected with African labour.

The widespread adoption in varying degrees of a system of administration which will utilize the tribal organization in its method of government makes increasingly important the influence of the returning worker upon the position and power of the native authority; it will obviously be futile to endeavour to strengthen and develop this authority while at the same time permitting the growth of an element which is constantly tending to weaken and discredit it. To the sympathetic European administrator, a chief may appear a fine and capable personality with the interests of his people genuinely at heart; to the home-coming wage-earner he may seem merely an ignorant and inexperienced old man engaged in a struggle to preserve obsolete and irritating restrictions. The degree to which this is likely to occur will, of course, depend largely on the difference in outlook and breadth of view between the native authority and his young critic. There would therefore seem much to be said in favour of the efforts made by some governments to furnish the future native rulers with a considerable measure of education and experience, so that they will be in a position to retain the respect of their more progressive and enterprising followers.

XVIII. WOMEN AND CHILD WORKERS

THE question of the position and safeguarding of women and child workers is one that has hitherto received somewhat scanty attention in Africa, owing to the small degree in which such labour exists as compared with European conditions. Factory employment being almost non-existent in comparison with other forms of work, there is not much opportunity for utilizing this type of labour except in agriculture or the attendant mechanical processes of preparing produce for export; the evils with which it has been necessary to cope in civilized communities are therefore hardly to be found.

There is, however, the possibility of women being indirectly employed, as carriers of the produce of their husbands' labours, or in other forms, when the temptation to earn additional money may withdraw them from home duties; this is a matter requiring special attention, since it is unlikely to be covered by any arrangements introduced to control direct employment.

The desire to ensure that African conditions are not inferior to those established elsewhere has led to increased attention being given to the matter, and the international conventions which control the use of such labour have been presented to the colonial powers for acceptance in their African possessions as much as for others. Thus legislation may be found which is really in advance of what might have been expected from the actual requirements of the situation, and precautions are sometimes established against evils which do not exist as yet.

Generally, women and children, when directly employed, will be found engaged in tasks such as weeding, coffee-picking, insect-gathering, and other light work, for which dexterity rather than strength is required. Employment is usually in the open air, and hours are short, often being left to the inclination of the worker by means of payment by result. Thus the possibility of unhygienic conditions and oppressive exploitation is reduced to a minimum, and female and juvenile workers will generally be found to enjoy favourable conditions.

They will probably consist of one of two classes: either local people who come to work daily, mostly at seasons when the harvest or other special call increases the demand for labourers, or the families of immigrant workers who are themselves employed on the estate.

In the case of the first of these classes, objectionable features are not likely to arise; the employees return to their villages each night, and travel to and fro in parties; tasks are completed in a leisurely fashion, and there is very little danger of overwork; while since this type of labour is most prominent during the seasons of greatest demand, there is probably no question of competition for jobs, and the employer must allow his people to carry out his requirements largely according to their inclination.

A proportion of youths may be found in the factories which produce the raw material, engaged in the lighter tasks there; in this case they may be the relatives of men who are performing the heavier duties, and will live in the labour lines with their relatives. As long as the work is suitable to their strength and ability, it is not likely that objection could be raised to this; there is, however, a tendency for the precocity and enterprise of the African boy to lead him into an attempt at something beyond his powers; it may thus occur that machines are tended or duties performed by youths who ought not to be entrusted with such responsibilities.

It is sometimes claimed that female employment leads to advantage being taken by overseers and others, and that the women's morals suffer; to this the reply is made that the conditions of the village are such that little restraint is exercised there, and that law and commerce cannot be unduly tender to excessive frailty.

With reference to juvenile employment, this may be criticized as tending to conflict with school attendance; this argument, however, naturally applies only where the school accommodation is adequate for the requirements of the population, a rare situation in Africa. In some cases, arrangements are made between the employers and the educational authorities whereby the holidays coincide with the short period during which the services of the pupils are needed, when there should be little likelihood of clashing.

The great popularity of education among Africans has led to an attempt to provide this on the part of some private employers; plantations are to be found where regular schools are maintained for adults as well as for the children of employees, while the Union Minière and the Huileries in the Congo provide quite an extensive education for their protégés; Portuguese colonial law goes farther, and contains provisions intended to compel the employer to provide teaching for any children on his estate.

It is also claimed that parents have a tendency to exploit the labour of their children, and that it is possible to find families where the adults depend on the earnings of the juveniles. It seems unlikely, however, that the African parent will have such a measure of authority over his child as to enable him to maintain such a state of affairs; rather it might be feared that the receipt of regular wages over which they have control may tend to make the young people unduly independent and undisciplined.

The various aspects of the employment of females and juveniles have been increasingly dealt with by means of the introduction of the appropriate European legislation, and it will thus be found that hours of employment, conditions of work, school attendance, compensation, and kindred questions, have already been regulated although in advance of actual requirements. Since the employment of women seems likely to figure only to a very small degree for a considerable time to come, some recent regulations may remain redundant for many years; in other instances, however, the need is more pressing. In particular, the employment of women shortly before and after childbirth well deserves the attention of the reformer; unfortunately, however, the usual African custom is in this particular deleterious, and a radical change will be required in this matter, not only in the hours of employment for wages, but in the whole treatment of the subject of maternity. Most of the more recent codes now require a clear month of unemployment both before and after childbirth, but the extent to which such provisions will admit of enforcement is doubtful. It should also not be overlooked that the larger undertakings in many cases maintain hospitals and child welfare centres at which the mother and baby can receive treatment and care far in advance of anything that could be hoped for in any native village; so that to this degree the fact of employment is definitely beneficial. It is to be presumed that progress will continue as a greater degree of organization and supervision of the employees becomes possible.

The question of the age at which children are to be allowed to accept work has produced considerable controversy as it did in Europe; the more recent appearance of the problem has, however, ensured that it has been treated on modern lines, and there has been no reproduction of the gradual raising of the age of employment from the shockingly low one which obtained in Europe in the last century. As soon as legislation on the point was contemplated at all, the suggested age was about 12, and there is a tendency for this to be raised to 14, with special restrictions for night work and for arduous forms of employment, when the age of admission may be as high as 18 years. Numerous people who have practical experience of the matter claim, however, that the raising of the age may be by no means beneficial to the child; they point out that the collecting of a tinful of insect pests, or the picking of a small quantity of coffee-berries, can hardly be termed work at all, and that such occupation is at least better than idleness; since school accommodation is almost certainly inadequate, the child has no rival claim on his time, and something likely to inculcate habits of industry may thus be advantageous. The position is undeniably different from that found in Europe, and the attempt to apply regulations suited to the latter is one that merits careful consideration before action is taken.

The question of night work is again one that has aspects which differ widely from those of Europe; in that continent, employment during the hours of darkness is almost always under unpleasant conditions, while in addition there are social objections to it. In Africa, on the contrary, it may well occur that the cool night, lit by a tropical moon, is by far the pleasantest time in which to work, and the native recognizes this by holding dances and social gatherings then, resting during the noonday heat. It thus follows that the absence from a code of rules on this point is by no means indicative of any omission.

In all these matters, however, the difficulty lies chiefly in the enforcement; the African boy is often intelligent and enterprising to a degree that makes him very suitable for some types of work, especially with machinery, on which the law prohibits his employment; connivance on the part of the employer is therefore highly probable, and complete detection of illegalities of this type would require an army of inspectors. Generally, however, really objectionable instances of child employment seem most unlikely to occur; the natural precocity and independence of the African child, and the real kindliness of his parents, alone suffice to render 'sweating' very improbable.

The moral aspect of the employment of women and children is one that at present hardly admits of legislative treatment; the low standard obtaining among many tribes, and the difficulty of supervision, render legal regulation unsuitable to the requirements of the position. It would seem rather a matter for educational authorities and missionaries to deal with, the law being restricted to adequate precautions against definitely undesirable conditions.

XIX. THE WAGE-EARNER AND THE LAND

Previous chapters have been devoted to the study of the connexion between the wage-earner and his home village, with the effect upon each of the work-seeking habit. It now remains to investigate the position of the labourer in his capacity of tribesman, with corresponding right to the land held by his people.

Consideration will emphasize the importance of this connexion, and since it is bound up with the welfare and contentment of the worker it will merit full examination.

In no part of the world has it proved possible so to regulate industry as to ensure steady employment without fluctuation, and the variations in the numbers required according to season and markets have entailed engagements or discharges affecting the general body of available labour. Periods of depression have resulted in lack of employment for large numbers, with consequent distress and need for relief; occasional spells of prosperity have absorbed possibly nearly all the labour available in the locality. More and more in Europe, however, there has been a tendency for the supply of labour to exceed the demand, and unemployment relief has been a problem of increasing seriousness, culminating in the world-wide depression of 1931. In addition to provision for those out of work, there has been the kindred question of support for those incapacitated by old age, sickness, or injury, while the need for meeting the requirements of the workers' children has also arisen. Arrangements of increasing complication and cost have been made in the various European countries, and these problems bid fair to dominate the political horizon among the more industrialized peoples.

How then have these difficulties been met in Africa? It is true that they have so far not arisen in a serious form, and that it has not hitherto been necessary to adopt any advanced measures to deal with them; nevertheless, they already exist in embryo, and are likely to increase in importance.

That the situation has not been more serious is due to two facts; the usual excess of demand over supply in the matter of labour which characterizes the normal African market, and the close connexion of the worker with the land.

Earlier in this work the flow of labour has been analysed, and some attempt has been made to picture the worker as he leaves his village to seek employment for a definite period, or accepts a daily wage on some enterprise near his home. In each case he is still based on his village and tribe, and he thus remains a land-holder even though this characteristic may be temporarily in abeyance.

It must also be remembered that in very many of the larger areas of employment it is the practice to provide both food and accommodation, the wage thus becoming an extra from which very little need really be spent, since it is not utilized in supporting a family. In the case of the daily worker, he is also a peasant proprietor, with the same fields that normally support him and his family; he has thus fairly adequate provision against need, should this arise.

The question of maintenance of unemployed therefore scarcely arises; if depression causes a general reduction in the numbers employed, the discharged workmen return to their homes and continue cultivation as they did before the advent of European enterprise. There will be little or no money for the purchase of luxuries, and government revenue in the shape of tax may suffer from the shortage of cash, but of actual hardship there will be little, unless a bad harvest should coincide with low prices for raw material. It is thus possible for the African labour market to absorb surprising quantities of discharged men without the widespread distress that would be caused in Europe; so long as the surplus hands are able to return to their homes, they will become self-supporting there, since the normal life of the village community, with its sowing and harvesting, has continued as usual in their absence.

It was thus possible in the general crisis of 1930-1 for discharges to take place on a very large scale in all the African countries producing raw material, without any great hardship resulting; in certain areas temporary difficulties arose, but where machinery existed to facilitate the return of the workers to their homes a solution was speedily reached.

The importance of a contractual right to provision for the return journey is thus emphasized; unless this has been previously guaranteed by the employer, a government may find itself faced with the necessity for furnishing assistance to large numbers of men discharged without the means to get to their homes, and without legal claim on any one.

Similarly, the village community cultivating its own land affords a solution of the problem of the disposal of the aged or incapacitated worker; the bountiful fertility of Africa usually enables him to be absorbed into tribal life without the burden of his support being appreciable, except where good land is scarce. In a previous chapter the difficulties of assessing and administering compensation for disablement were discussed; it is a most fortunate feature of the problem that there is the natural solution afforded by the return to tribal life.

In contrast with the condition of affairs described above, there are certain areas of Africa where primitive conditions have largely passed away; increasing development has led to restriction of tribal lands, while in some cases considerable sections of the native population have been permanently alienated from their old territories. There has thus arisen a class which has no right to any land under old Bantu law, but lives either as some form of 'squatter' or forms part of an urban or rural population entirely dependent on wage-earning for its support. There is also the community to be found in the neighbourhood of some large undertaking, such as an important mining centre, which consists of permanent employees of the company, looking to it for their entire support, and cut off from the village homes from which they originally sprang.

It is obvious that such people will lack the protection against misfortune afforded by access to the land; the detribalized worker must face destitution if he loses the employment from which he draws his wages, and will become a homeless wanderer picking up a precarious living for himself and his family as best he can. The danger of creating such a class is very real, for they must form a miserable and discontented body almost inevitably inclined to crime, while their misfortunes will render them peculiarly responsive to any agitator or mischief-maker.

It therefore seems clear that when circumstances are such that the evolution of a class of landless wage-earners is inevitable, the situation must be faced and provision prepared for the relief of possible unemployment and the care of those no longer able to work.

Without this, the state will have to deal with a dangerous element of embittered semi-criminals of a type that forms a standing menace to good order and prosperity. Particularly is this true of urban communities, where slums may arise which are centres of crime, vice, and disease; pass-laws and police control may reduce the evil, but the only real remedy would seem to be to provide beforehand for such people, instead of resting content with measures which merely transfer the weight of the problem from the towns to the country.

The permanent employee of the great company is more happily situated, since he is seldom turned adrift; in many cases, the provision made for such dependants is very complete, and both workers and families have their needs catered for to a surprising degree. It must not be overlooked, however, that such enterprises, in encouraging numbers of natives to detach themselves from tribal life and lose their connexion with the land, are accepting considerable responsibilities; if they reproduce European conditions, they will find it necessary to deal with resultant difficulties, and a careful government will take steps to ensure that they do not shirk their obligations.

The 'squatter' presents a peculiar and difficult problem of his own, on which very much might be written. It is, however, more a question of land tenure than of labour, and for that reason the matter will here be dealt with only in so far as it affects the workman.

The 'squatter' is to be met with in various forms, originating in widely different circumstances. The earliest instances were afforded by tribesmen whose land had been granted to other occupants, and who clung on to their former possessions with the permission of the new owners; in many cases the land was not required immediately, and there was thus no necessity for disturbance, a working agreement being arrived at whereby the native remained in occupation in return for certain services. A commoner instance is that of the employee on a farm who has brought his family with him and settled on a small piece of land granted to him by the owner; primarily a regular wage-earner, he may become a part-time worker, and divide his energies between his landlord's property and his own ground, according to the informal agreement between them. Another type is the dependant of a large undertaking such as a mine, who lives on the company's property and cultivates their land, on condition that he performs so many days' work per annum, or supplies a stipulated amount of food from his garden; this type is easily evolved from the ordinary worker who has been in the first instance granted permission to cultivate a small patch of ground.

In all these cases the principal difficulty arises from the insecurity of the tenure, though there are other complications; there is always the possibility that the land in question may be needed for other purposes, when the 'squatter' must be dispossessed; on the other hand, he frequently becomes unsatisfactory in the performance of his obligation, when the threat of eviction will be held over his head to enable him to be replaced by some one more satisfactory. Again, an unscrupulous landlord may take advantage of good work put into virgin soil to expel the occupant in order to profit by his toil in development. On the other hand, the owner may be reluctant to deprive the tenant of his holding, even though the return rendered is worth very little; the unpopularity of such an act, and the possibility of sympathetic action on the part of other workers, may make even an inclement landlord hesitate. It is clear that the position is one that needs careful regulation and support by law where it exists.

The system has been regarded with suspicion by administrators for many years, owing to the difficulties to which it gives rise; popular among agricultural communities in some cases, on account of its partial solution of labour problems, it has seldom met with much favour from governments. Early Dutch laws in South Africa were directed to a stringent limitation of the number of 'squatters' on any one farm, and numerous later instances could be quoted of action to the same effect; usually measures have been taken to regularize the terms of the tenancy and furnish a reasonable amount of protection to the temporary occupant of the land in the form of security against harsh or uncompensated disturbance. This may serve to reduce the cases of injustice in connexion with the system, and may render its working comparatively innocuous, but it entirely overlooks the wider aspect of the practice, in encouraging the creation of a landless class of native. It is obvious that no really permanent right can be given to the tenant, and that cases may frequently arise where land is required which is temporarily occupied by families who have resided on it for a considerable period and regard it as their home. If then they should be dispossessed, they will be unlikely to have retained any right to the old tribal lands, and they must therefore set out to seek a holding elsewhere; reserves may be already well occupied, and their plea for a share will be met unsympathetically by the native authorities. They drift about, possibly to find accommodation on another piece of private property, or perhaps to swell the numbers of an embryo slum population. The danger of increasing such an element in the community is too serious to be regarded lightly by any government; the question is one that needs careful consideration especially in its early stages.

To summarize the foregoing review, it seems clear that the retention of the connexion between the worker and the land will in a large measure afford a substitute in Africa for the elaborate provisions required in Europe to meet the needs of the wage-dependent population. As long as the displaced worker can if necessary be re-absorbed into tribal life, provision for unemployment, old age pensions, and similar obligations of modern industrialized society will be largely superfluous; if, however, a considerable class of landless manual workers be created, and European conditions reproduced, the government concerned will sooner or later be compelled to recognize the inevitability of appropriate measures to meet the attendant problems.

XX. LABOUR AND INTERNATIONAL RELATIONS

IN all parts of Africa development is stimulating the movement of labour across the international borders, and hardly any country now exists which is neither an importer nor an exporter of labour; the balance is constantly shifting, and the tide which sets in one direction for some years may be turned elsewhere by a counter-attraction; a series of maps illustrating the flow at the beginning of each of the last few decades would indicate numerous changes and innovations.

It is therefore remarkable that very little appears to have been done towards establishing some sort of agreement on policy between the countries mainly affected; various arrangements have been made to govern the supply of labour between neighbouring territories, and the Union of South Africa has entered into a series of agreements with the authorities of Portuguese East Africa regarding the flow of workers from there to the mines; the Belgian Congo has drawn men from Angola to meet its needs, and various other minor understandings have been concluded in other parts where the flow of labour rendered this desirable. These, however, all concern the number of men to be permitted to go, their treatment while at work, their eventual repatriation, and similar questions; any settlement of general policy in the matter of the status and social position of the worker appears to have been avoided.

It seems inevitable that something of this kind will have to be attempted in the near future, if the migration of labour is not to become a factor threatening disruption of the settled policy of certain countries; anomalies and discrepancies already exist, and only the ignorance and apathy of the African has permitted their continuance without friction; the growth of education and the widespread tendency towards solidarity must increasingly threaten industrial peace.

The most conspicuous and probably the most urgent of these problems is to be found in the Union of South Africa. There a large white population established for centuries has led to an appreciable risk of inter-racial competition for the better paid tasks, and the existence of a considerable body of 'poor whites' has long perplexed a government already harassed by friction between British and Dutch; the danger of a gradual swamping of the European skilled artisan by a lower paid African has thus created a fear of the eventual overwhelming of the white population.

Trade union rules have therefore strongly reinforced government action in an effort to eliminate competition between the races, and these have been upheld by public opinion to a degree that has made them very effective; many tasks are rigidly restricted to Europeans, and the African artisan finds it difficult to obtain training and teaching, and almost impossible to secure employment when he has achieved proficiency. He must therefore rest content with the wage of a manual worker of elementary type, employed under the control of a white man whose job he might possibly be quite able to perform himself, but to which he can never aspire. As it has been put, 'the black man's ceiling is the white man's floor' in the matter of wages; the curious position being thus created that the European trade union and labour element, elsewhere the protagonist of the native's cause, is found strongly defending the colour bar in industry.

Such a situation has been vigorously attacked as being unjust and degrading; its permanent maintenance is declared to be impossible, and it is therefore represented as a growing danger to the State to which its eventual breakdown represents a grave peril.

To this it is replied that the objection is not to the black man as such, but to his standard of living; he notoriously is content with far poorer conditions than those of the European, and can tolerate circumstances much inferior to those considered essential for the white man. If therefore he were permitted to flood the market for skilled labour, a general lowering of wages would result, with a corresponding depression of the standard of living; the 'poor white' class would be reinforced to make room for a number of Africans negligible when compared with the total population, and a general degradation of conditions would ensue which would benefit no one but the capitalist employer, and would eventually prove harmful to the black, quite as much as to the white, worker. The existing state of affairs is thus stoutly defended in the interests of both races.

A somewhat similar position exists in Southern Rhodesia, where restrictions on the employment of skilled Africans are also to be found, for much the same reasons, and it is to be presumed that something of the kind will also arise in Northern Rhodesia as agriculture wanes in importance before mining developments.

It is not proposed to discuss the degree to which such a policy is justifiable or feasible as a permanency; rather, its conflict with the position existing in neighbouring countries will be studied.

To the north of the Union and the Rhodesias is the rapidly progressing Belgian Congo, where rich mines draw large numbers of workers; in addition, the railway forms an important means of communication and ensures a perpetual flow of travellers. It is thus of great importance to the southern countries that the Congo maintains no colour distinction in the matter of employment, and that the African there can obtain work at any task for which he is fitted; more, he can secure training for such positions and subsequently has no difficulty in earning good wages. This state of affairs may be applauded as fair treatment of the African, or condemned as capitalistic exploitation of cheap labour; whichever view is taken, the position has to be recognized.

It thus occurs that the train from the south reaches the Belgian border with a staff that is European in all the important posts; there the traveller changes to a train which is managed almost entirely by Africans, the various stations being similarly controlled. Thereafter, the contrast is sustained, and in all directions Africans can be found doing tasks which would be prohibited to them farther south.

The change in this case is sufficiently conspicuous to attract the attention of the most superficial observer; there are, however, other anomalies on the borders.

There is an annual influx from Portuguese East Africa to the Rand amounting to many thousands, and these men must notice the difference in the attitude of the two governments of which they have experience; the conspicuous colour bar of the Union must contrast strangely with the entire lack of it in the Portuguese territory, and even if the latter is not sufficiently advanced to offer much opening for the ambitious African, the difference in the situation must excite comment.

Nyasaland, again, presents a conflicting element; education has been pressed forward among an enterprising people to a degree that has resulted in the production of far more partially educated natives than can be employed in their homes. These therefore

wander further afield seeking work, too often unfortunately insufficiently trained to be of much value, but nevertheless ambitious
for advancement. They are to be found in the Union, in the
Congo, throughout Tanganyika territory, and even farther away,
usually in clerical or other non-manual employment, while they
contribute a quota to the floating population of the towns.

Tanganyika, on account of the Mandate, is prohibited from
establishing any colour preference, and the African worker can
secure any work for which he is fitted; here, however, a further
complication arises in the shape of the Indian artisan. The latter
forms an intermediate class between the well-paid European and
the ill-trained African; drawing a far higher wage than the latter
on account of his greater skill, he views with jealousy the tendency
of the native to increase his efficiency and replace the Asiatic.
Combination along racial lines tends to arise, and the traveller
must be still further bewildered at the contrasting conditions
which he finds. The economic and sociological arguments in
favour of the position in the Union will be almost always beyond
the grasp of the African, who must therefore contrast the opportunities offered him in the neighbouring countries with a resultant
tendency to regard the Union flag as a symbol of oppression. Thus
a powerful additional element of friction is added to a racial
position already fraught with dangerous potentialities.

Farther north a similar interchange is taking place; Uganda
draws her labour for cotton-picking largely from over the Congo
border; the native coffee-planters of Bukoba also rely largely on
this source. Belgian railways in the Congo have been to a great
extent built by labour from Angola; British West Africa recruits
from French territory in many cases; Italian Somaliland depends
on the Sudan, and in every direction large numbers are in constant
movement over the international borders. Boundaries are in most
cases arbitrary as far as the African is concerned, and he regards
the flag under which he works merely as an indication of the sort
of treatment which he may expect.

The degree to which the African is not only travelling, but also
observing, is probably not generally recognized; it is, however,
easy to hear a camp-fire conversation in the Congo during which
conditions in the Union, Rhodesia, Tanganyika, and Angola are
all discussed and commented upon; brothers from Nyasaland may
go, one to the north and the other to the south, and may be trusted

to compare their experiences on their return home. The advent of the motor-car and its use for long overland journeys has afforded another means for the African to secure employment which will give him wide and varied opportunities for observation.

The growth of education, again, has greatly facilitated inter-communication and consequent comparison of conditions; the native publications of the Union—often advanced and bitter in tone—are to be met even north of the Equator, and there is a constant and growing stream of letters carrying news between widely separated relatives and friends. At present, no doubt, the elementary degree of education possessed by such people precludes very much serious discussion by post or in the press; the tendency is there, however, and must inevitably grow.

In addition to what may be termed the political aspect of the situation, there are other complications created by the inter-territorial migrations. Disease is inevitably disseminated; customs barriers are additionally strained; police measures become increasingly difficult; currency questions are involved; revenue is affected, and the normal food supply may be suddenly jeopardized by an influx from across the border.

Laws in many cases conflict. The Rhodesian requirement of the retention of deferred wages is diametrically opposed to that of Tanganyika on this point; Portugal permits the payment of a *per capita* sum to chiefs for recruits, while this is strictly prohibited in the neighbouring British territories; Kenya enforces a strict pass law while Tanganyika dispenses with any such measure; Angola insists on Portuguese as a means of instruction, though the Congo accepts Swahili and other native languages; and conscription of military type in French territory may render British West Africa more attractive.

Recruiting regulations also vary greatly, with the result that in many cases there is a great incentive to an enterprising labour agent to station himself near the border in order to resort to practices prohibited for his rivals in the country concerned, but permissible where he is; the activities of such a man may cause great annoyance to the neighbouring administration, who will nevertheless be practically powerless to deal with him.

Such conflict of practice and policy must perplex the African greatly, and it is easy to see how prejudicial his conclusions may be in some cases; human nature, whatever the colour of its skin, tends to dwell upon the shortcomings rather than the benefits of a government, and a growing volume of criticism must be expected from the travelled and experienced native who resents some measure of restraint for which he can see no justification.

Some attempt has been made at times to restrict the flow, so as to segregate certain populations and shield them from what is regarded as dangerous contamination. Belief in the efficacy or practicability of such measures is most unlikely to survive actual investigation of the problem; the ring fence policy can hardly hope for serious advocacy in the face of present conditions, though change has been so rapid that it is not unnatural that the older generation has failed to observe its extent.

Plainly, labour movements when affecting international boundaries are the intimate concern of both governments; it is thus essential that both should be alive to the importance of the possibilities. An apathetic attitude on the part of either will prevent the supply of statistics and information which are essential for the administration of the other, while even more serious results will arise if proper control and observation are not available to guard against the occurrence of disease, famine, or other trouble.

In view of the importance of the problem and its many ramifications, it seems remarkable that greater efforts have not been made towards interterritorial discussions and agreements; these seem, however, to have been rarely attempted and very restricted in scope even when arranged.

XXI. SOME ASPECTS OF INVESTIGATION

THE attempt to survey the general conditions governing wage-earning in Africa is now complete; the primitive mentality of the worker has been examined, his history has been recapitulated in so far as it may affect his response to the impact of the capitalistic system, and the circumstances in which he is recruited and employed have been reviewed. It now remains to consider the points to which attention might be directed with a view to arriving at an estimate of the real effect of the acquirement of the wage-earning habit on a tribe.

It is clear that this will involve elaborate investigations continued over a long period, and requiring the assistance of persons of various qualifications; the development of social and administrative services in most parts of Africa is at present hardly adequate for such a purpose, and it may well be that governments would find themselves unable to attempt such research without the support of scientific bodies. The importance of the problem might, however, justify such a combination of effort, at any rate for limited areas of special suitability, since the results obtained would be of outstanding value, and of a type that has hitherto scarcely been attempted in its entirety. Such research being the object of the Major Plan of the International Institute of African Languages and Cultures, co-operation might be arranged which would permit of the necessary supplementing of limited government resources, with a view to co-ordination of effort in a scheme of thorough investigation.

It may therefore be useful to survey the requirements of such an inquiry, without reference to the feasibility of such an undertaking with the means now in existence in the various countries considered.

It is suggested that the most suitable material would be afforded by a tribe that has not yet emerged from the primitive stage, and which is only beginning to acquire the wage-earning habit; the effect of the latter could then be studied as it increases in influence on the community, and the resultant modifications, improvements, or disadvantages, could be assessed at their proper value.

A preliminary survey on ethnological and sociological lines will be needed, in order to secure a picture of the primitive state of the people; their character and qualities according to their race-group will have to be borne in mind, and the degree to which they have already advanced on their own initiative should be carefully noted. Tribal organization and discipline will also be of interest, together with such customs as may affect the physical or moral well-being of the people.

Medical particulars will be of great importance, and the collection of vital statistics must be attempted as far as possible. The food-supply of the people, its variety and deficiencies, with the effect observable, will require careful noting, with special reference to the vitamin content; the obscurer forms of deficiency diseases and the suspected effects of under-nourishment will be included. The birth-rate will require close examination, and an effort will be necessary to secure figures as far as possible accurate, showing the position under primitive conditions; the percentage of children per head, with notes on stillbirth, miscarriage, or abortion, will form a basis of comparison with the results to be secured later.

Diseases already prevalent must be recorded, with especial reference to venereal affections; careful examination of the average males, with a view to discovering their initial susceptibility to disease of the lungs, should not be omitted. Physical measurements will present little difficulty, at any rate as far as the males are concerned, and tables of average weight, height, and principal measurements can be compiled with fair reliability.

When as much as possible of the foregoing information has been secured, a record will have been obtained which will admit of comparison with the results to be accumulated in the course of years; without a detailed picture of the primitive condition of the tribe, the effect of future development cannot be accurately assessed.

As then the people begin to leave home to seek work at a distance, a large measure of supervision will be necessary; while this need not be irksome, it should be as thorough as is feasible, and results should be carefully tabulated. The method of recruiting adopted will presumably lend itself to accurate record, while medical inspection will provide valuable data as to the condition of the men when leaving home. Those who leave without entering into any contract (if this be permitted) may introduce a certain element of uncertainty, but this may admit of compensation. Details should at any rate be procurable from the tribal authorities, and a voluntary submission to medical inspection might prove attainable. Particular heed will be paid to the period of time for which the men are absent, and the checking of the date of return will be an important feature; a second medical inspection on arrival from work would be of the greatest value, and should be attempted as far as possible.

Efforts should be made to confine employment to a strictly limited number of places where the conditions are fully known, and where the necessary staff for observations is available. The rationing of the workers will be of great interest, especially if it can be arranged for the diet scale to include such articles as may replace any deficiency normally existing in the tribal food-supply. Medical examination of the men while employed, with statistics of mortality and sickness, will of course be essential.

Information should also be secured as to the climate of the place of employment, the local diseases existing there, the variety of food procurable in addition to a ration issue, while any particulars of the habits and customs of local tribes likely to affect visitors will be of value. Details of the type of housing provided, with accommodation for bathing, &c., will also be collected. Finally, the percentage of men who go to work accompanied by their women will be carefully noted, and details must also be secured showing the degree to which promiscuous relationships are entered into.

When a sufficient period has elapsed to make the effects of the migration of labourers perceptible, it will be possible to observe the results both on the men concerned and on the life of the village.

The most obvious feature will probably be the difference in physique of the returned recruits; given that conditions of employment have been suitably selected and well maintained, a noticeable improvement should result; medical examination will indicate the exact degree to which this has taken place. On the other hand, it may be found that certain deleterious effects have occurred, in the shape of diseases such as hookworm, malaria, or other infections previously unknown in the village, while venereal contamination may also have to be reckoned with.

Interest will attach to observations as to the extent to which the improved conditions of housing or sanitation experienced while at work are reflected at all in the future mode of life in the village; appetite for a wider variety of food may also be expected.

The mental changes produced will deserve attention; the articles carried back from work, as well as those for which some demand springs up in the local stores, are worth remark, while any effort towards thrift in disposing of earnings would merit special note. Of greater importance will be the attitude of the travellers towards their tribal authorities and their old customs, with particular reference to marriage; how far may imported ideas tend to break down the former family life?

In the village itself a change will grow more perceptible as the periodical exodus becomes an established habit, and this will furnish the justification or condemnation of the wage-earning system for that tribe. Vital statistics will be of outstanding importance, and the births will give a most valuable index of improvement or the reverse. Information will be needed as to the degree to which wives remain attached to their absent husbands, or how far such separations tend to disrupt the family; the actual number of births taking place, and the proportion of miscarriages and stillbirths will also have to be obtained as accurately as conditions admit; infantile mortality will require most careful attention, with a view to possible benefits accruing from improved feeding on the part of the parents.

The life of the community will have to be observed, and the vitality of tribal organization established. Changes will be inevitable, but are these on sound and intelligent lines, or are they limited to a sort of agnostic denial of all authority, with consequent breaking down of the established structure of native society? The views of the tribal chiefs and elders should be carefully ascertained.

If such a set of observations could be carried out over a period of some five years or more, it would result in a most valuable contribution to African sociology; with such data at hand, it would be possible to determine exactly how far the wage-earning habit affected the tribe; the resultant advantages or defects would be apparent, and steps could be taken to eliminate evil results as far as possible, while utilizing the benefits for the steady improvement of the tribe.

An investigation of this elaborate nature would of course entail very considerable work for a number of people; there is no record of anything of this sort available at present, and the necessary machinery hardly exists. Various demographic records have been made in certain countries, sometimes involving much work over long periods; unfortunately, they have too often omitted to take adequate account of the annual exodus of the work-seekers, with the result that the conclusions are valueless for practical purposes. The growth of recruiting in an area may have most important effects on the local vital statistics, especially the birth-rate, and the failure to take this into account not only vitiates the value of the conclusions, but renders the supporting statistics dangerously misleading.

To collect the necessary information, it will be needful to secure the co-operation of all available observers; to the general supervision of the administrative officer, and the detailed statistics of the doctor, must be added the local knowledge of the missionary and the practical experience of the planter and trader; similar work will be required simultaneously at the place of employment, while information as to travelling conditions *en route*, &c., will also be needed. Some centre for the combination of these results will be required, and the material should be submitted to the best available brains for analysis.

It is not suggested that such detailed inquiry will be feasible or even necessary in any but selected cases; it will, however, be increasingly important for the various aspects of the problem to receive attention, so that a well-based opinion as to the progress of the native community may be formed. At present even the elements of such information are often found to be lacking, and although genuine grounds for uneasiness as to the welfare of a particular tribe may exist, no evidence can be found on which to base definite conclusions or formulate remedial measures.

With the data available on the completion of an investigation such as is suggested, it would be possible to utilize the more limited information available for other areas, in order to detect undesirable developments in their early stages; exact and detailed particulars relating to one tribe would serve to indicate the tendencies existing elsewhere, with suggestions for corrective measures advisable. The study would, in fact, provide a much-needed standard whereby to form an opinion of the general trend of development, and it would throw light on numerous problems at present only vaguely perceived. It is scarcely necessary to stress the practical and economic value of any investigation of the labour market; the inquiry would thus be of real material importance, apart from its administrative and ethical implications.

It is hoped that the foregoing study of the various aspects of the introduction of the capitalistic system of wage-earning into Africa will serve to draw attention to the importance of the subject, and its great potentialities, both for good and evil, in the future of the continent.

PART II

SUMMARY OF LEGISLATION
PREFATORY NOTE

THE following summary of the laws of various African countries is intended as a guide to the nature and scope of the legislation, with references to facilitate consultation of the originals. As classification and method of arrangement vary widely with the governments concerned, each section has been drawn up so as to accord mainly with local practice; the principal features have been presented under suitable headings, in order to simplify reference.

The laws which are in force in each country have been summarized, without any analysis of the degree to which they are actually applied; in this matter, investigation will show a very wide variation, and in some cases the divergence between theory and practice is great.

While every effort has been made to render the summary comprehensive and accurate, it does not claim to be exhaustive or authoritative; since its compilation entailed the examination, not only of all laws, ordinances, and decrees, but also the relevant proclamations, notices, &c., based on them, for each country under consideration, certain errors and omissions have probably occurred. Where these are detected, the author would much appreciate notification, to enable correction to be made.

The latest information available has as far as possible been embodied; in the case of certain countries, however, this is no later than the beginning of 1931.

LIST OF AFRICAN COUNTRIES DEALT WITH IN THE FOLLOWING SUMMARY OF LEGISLATION

LEGISLATION throughout the Belgian Congo on labour is on important points the same; there are, however, certain modifications in the various provinces, applied according to local requirements, in view of the different conditions obtaining in each locality, and the varying degrees of advancement. The stagnation of development during the War, and the subsequent rapid progress, resulted in the creation of labour problems of comparatively recent date; legislation on the subject is consequently mostly post-war, and it has accumulated especially in the past few years.

In 1932 regulations dealing in detail with labour were introduced, but the situation resulting from the speed at which development was proceeding appeared so grave that two commissions were appointed, one in 1924 and the second in 1928, to make full examination, with subsequent recommendations. These commissions investigated the position in detail; the personnel was numerous and influential, and the resultant conclusions were of interest and importance, not only in the Congo, but beyond its borders.

In particular, the first attempt in Africa was made to compile an economic and sociological survey of a whole colony, and the potentialities of the various regions with reference to their capacity for progress, with particular regard to the labour available for the various enterprises contemplated. A careful investigation was made to ascertain the proportion of the population which could be recruited without resultant harm to the welfare of the native communities. The existing situation was considered to be alarming, in view of the probable early exhaustion of labour resources, and the evil effects likely to be suffered by the native population. Certain principles were laid down, and the importance was stressed of a preliminary survey before development was permitted in fresh directions. The committees recommended the adoption of a detailed programme for each region, to be adhered to without deviation; the organization of labour recruitment throughout the country so as to ensure the best utilization of all resources; and special efforts to promote the introduction of mechanical devices of all kinds tending to economize labour.

The permissible percentages for recruitment without risk of

injury to the well-being of the native communities were considered to be as follows: of the adult working population, 5 per cent. might be sent to distant places of employment; another 5 per cent. might be employed in localities not involving a complete severing of family life, that is to say, within two days' march of the home village; and an additional 15 per cent. would then be available for employment in the neighbourhood of their homes. The Commission thus considered 25 per cent. as the maximum proportion of the adult able-bodied population which might be withdrawn from normal native village life without resultant harm to tribal welfare; they found that in certain regions this figure had already been exceeded.

The recommendations of the Commission of 1928 resulted in the delimitation of economic zones in the various provinces, in certain of which further concessions and continued recruiting were prohibited, while in the others a full examination of the position was carried out with the help of employers and missionaries, with a view to determining the future policy. The Committee stressed the danger of an official recommendation or encouragement to work being regarded by the natives as an order, and advised that government employees should be freed from all responsibility for furthering a labour supply ('Cette situation provoque un malaise auquel on ne pourrait mettre fin qu'en déchargeant explicitement les agents de l'autorité de toute responsabilité dans la situation de main-d'œuvre des entreprises européennes'). Officials should limit their activities to the encouragement of work-seeking by legitimate means, and the supervision of recruiting methods.

The Annual Report on the Administration of the Belgian Congo for 1928 indicated the attention being given to the whole question of the effect of the demand for labour; the programme for the future was summarized as follows: (1) the repopulation of unduly depleted areas, and the discouragement of any further exodus; (2) the encouragement of recruiting in areas hitherto untapped; (3) the exercise of caution in the granting of any further concessions; (4) the rationing of labour to employers, limiting them to the number demonstrably necessary; (5) the development of the Labour Department; (6) the encouragement of mechanization; (7) the adoption of further measures for the protection of the workers and their families; (8) the extension of social services.

In a speech to the Chamber of Representatives February 21 and 27, 1929, M. Jaspar, Colonial Minister, detailed the measures taken for the protection of the native population against the evils of too rapid development. These may be summarized as follows: The whole territory has been divided into zones; first, those in which industries can no longer be established, nor concessions granted; second, those in which only agricultural concessions may be granted; and third, free zones. There are to be no new mining concessions for an indeterminate period; the largest part of the country is closed to all new enterprises; the zones in which new concessions may still be granted is reduced to one-ninth of the whole area; in one-third of the country, only concessions for agriculture or stock-raising may be granted. All new grants are made subject to the following stipulations: (1) the finding of labour locally; (2) the introduction of the use of labour-saving machinery; (3) the proving of technical and financial resources commensurate with the importance of the undertaking; (4) the allocation of a portion of the capital to hygiene and education for the benefit of the native population.

The Annual Report for 1929 estimates the success attending these measures, and furnishes details of the various zones in each province. The safe percentage of work-seeking emigrants had been surpassed in a number of cases, but improvement was generally indicated, the excess being nowhere great. The proportion of men travelling with their families had also increased, thanks to the efforts of the employing companies.

Legislation was early introduced to regulate the use of labour derived from the militia levy; the Decree of June 3, 1906, amended by that of February 16, 1910, authorized the carrying out of public works by the second section of the annual levy; the latter Decree fixed the maximum period for which such labour might be required at three years. In practice, however, this right has not been enforced for a considerable period, and refusals to sanction its application have become the rule. In 1920 the Colonial Minister and Council refused to approve of a levy of 1,000 workers for railway construction, while in August 1926 they declined to sanction a levy of 9,000 natives for the construction of the Matadi Railway. Workers are to be engaged on free contracts only, as in the case of private employers.

The right to *requisition* able-bodied adult males is, however, reserved to administrative officers by the Decree of December 26, 1922, which authorizes this for the provision of guides, porters, or paddlers; only urgent need justifies this, and the period of employment may not exceed fifteen days a month, or twenty-five days per annum; pay at the ruling local rate must be given.

The Decree of March 19, 1925, regulates the use of *porterage*, and empowers provincial governors to prohibit this in areas where other means of transport are available; in the Eastern and Katanga Provinces this was applied by Ordinances 42 of June 25, 1925, and 37 of December 3, 1925, respectively; offences are punishable with a fine of 1,000 francs.

Forced labour may be levied in special circumstances by the administrative officer in charge of a district (administrateur territorial), to combat infectious diseases, famine, or emergencies; it may also be used for the maintenance, for the exclusive benefit of the inhabitants, of cultivation of foodstuffs or exportable produce (Decree of May 2, 1910). The period of employment is limited to five days a month or sixty days a year. The Decree of July 18, 1918, provides a penalty of seven days' imprisonment and a fine of 200 francs in case of non-performance. The Ordinance of August 30, 1924, prescribes the method in which this agricultural levy is to be utilized, and requires a survey and report from the local administrative officers to the District Commissioner, for his sanction, before the work is begun.

(NOTE. The claim of the right to resort to compulsory labour in order to establish the cultivation of an exportable crop for the exclusive benefit of the inhabitants has been the subject of considerable discussion; it is the explanation of Belgium's reluctance to agree to the Geneva Draft Convention on Forced Labour of June 1930. The system is said to have produced excellent results in various parts of the Congo, in ameliorating the conditions of life of backward tribes, and in providing them with the means of enriching themselves by the produce of their own fields. It was severely criticized in the Belgian Chambre des Représentants, sessions of July 14 and 21, 1932.)

Failure to pay tax renders a native liable to arrest, when he can be employed on clearing of bush, roadwork, labour on government stations, or porterage (Ordinance of November 30, 1918).

The Ordinance of November 16, 1922, established a *Labour Office* in Leopoldville, and this arrangement was subsequently copied in other provinces, and further developed; Ordinance of June 18, 1930, provides for a provincial medical service for labour supervision, to assist the *Inspectors of Industry and Commerce*, and to apply to all commercial, industrial, or agricultural enterprises; where an Inspector is not available, the duties are to be undertaken by the local administrative officer. Labour hygiene is placed in charge of a government medical officer, with assistants, to be appointed directly by the Governor.

Recruiting is governed primarily by the Decree of March 16, 1922, but this has been reinforced and extended by provincial legislation. While conditions are not identical in all provinces, they are similar as regards the main features, the Katanga Ordinance of March 26, 1927, being perhaps the most detailed. Regulations apply not only to professional recruiters, but to all employers of more than ten servants, recruited from a distance of more than 25 kilos. from the place of employment.

The Decree regulates relations between a native, and an employer who is either a non-native, or a native paying a personal tax other than the usual native tax.

Recruiting is free, but a certain standard is required from those engaging in it; Article 42 authorizes the Governor to require a guarantee of from 400 to 40,000 francs.

The recruiter must provide the workman with a written statement showing the place and date of recruitment, place of employment, pay, and duration of contract; this must be signed by the recruiter and left in the possession of the workman. At this stage only a modified contract can be made, as a token of engagement ('contrat d'embauchage'); this requires the recruiter to provide work as promised, and the recruit to proceed to the place of employment and accept work as specified. An appearance before the local administrative officer is obligatory, and a list must be given to him in duplicate showing names and other particulars as given to the natives; this list is scrutinized and signed by the officer. The recruiter is liable for repatriation expenses until these become the liability of the employer.

The recruiter must furnish suitable *housing, food, and medical attention*, and such clothing as may be necessary; he cannot contract out of this liability, nor can it be replaced by a payment in money. The Decree of June 15, 1922, renders medical inspection obligatory.

On the *journey* to the place of employment, every party of twenty-five must be in charge of a conductor who will make the necessary arrangements for food and shelter; if the party numbers more than 250, the conductor must be a European; regulations refer to the disposal of any man who may fall sick on the journey, and make his safe repatriation a duty of the conductor. Precautions for the use of mechanical transport are detailed, the use of closed wagons being prohibited for long journeys of more than 150 kilometres. In the case of recruits for the Katanga, stricter rules apply; blanket and shirt must be supplied, and rations are detailed; on arrival, full particulars of all the recruits must be furnished to the Inspector of Industry, while a second medical inspection is also required. Transport of recruits must be by water or rail when possible, failing which certain approved routes must be followed, on which camps are established at not more than 30 kilometres apart. At each of these, an approved ration must be available, and at certain of them there must be a medical attendant approved by the Provincial Medical Officer.

On engagement, every recruit must be furnished with a *work-book* (*livret de travail*) by the employer, in which must be shown his name, village, chief, nature of work, time, and place of employment, wages, dates of payment, length of contract, and any other particulars required by the Governor. Fines, with the reason for infliction, must also be shown. The book must be left in the possession of the employee.

In the case of any engagement for more than three months, a visa from an official is necessary both for the contract and for the work-book; this certifies the proper comprehension of the terms by the contracting parties. No contract for more than three years is valid.

In case of *illness*, the employer is responsible for medical treatment until the end of the contract, if this is for more than fifteen days; for engagements shorter than fifteen days, the employer is liable for the same number of days as the duration of the contract. In case of accident, the employer is liable for a period twice as long as in the case of illness; the employee's claim to compensation is not thereby affected. During incapacity, the employee is entitled to quarter wages, or half wages where rations are not provided.

Wages must be paid in current coin; at not longer intervals than weekly in the case of servants not entitled to rations, monthly when food is supplied.

Penal Sanctions for Servants. Destroying or mutilating a work-book, 50 francs fine, or seven days' imprisonment. Fraudulently obtaining an advance, up to three months' imprisonment, with fine. Grave or repeated infringement of rules for labourers,

50 francs fine, or fifteen days' imprisonment. (NOTE: Corporal punishment cannot be inflicted for labour offences.)

For infringement of regulations, or loss or destruction of tools or materials, the employer may fine the servant up to one day's pay, or half a day's pay in cases where rations are not furnished.

Special officers termed *Inspectors of Industry* are charged with the maintenance of proper conditions of working and living. These include sanitation, safety, and convenience of buildings, the quantity and quality of rations, the lay-out and maintenance of camps or sleeping accommodation, the organization of medical attention, and the reporting of accidents. Infringement of any of these requirements renders the employer liable to a fine of 2,000 francs or one month's imprisonment.

The Ordinance of June 2, 1927, creates for each provincial Governor an *Advisory Council* of Labour and Industry (Comité consultatif du travail et de l'industrie) to consider and recommend measures for the improvement of labour conditions generally; this is composed of five officials and five nominated prominent local non-officials.

Ordinance 22 of May 28, 1930, for the Katanga Province, introduced somewhat stricter provisions for the care of labourers; camps of acclimatization must be established where recruits are to be kept for twenty-eight days (fourteen days in the case of re-employment) engaged on light tasks and under special supervision and medical inspection.

Ordinance No. 55 of the Governor-General June 18, 1930, introduced stricter provisions generally, provided for the appointment of Government Medical Officers to collaborate with the Inspectors of Industry, and required a certificate of physical fitness for every employee, to be recorded in his work-book.

Construction of camps is regulated, and the maximum duration of one year is introduced for grass huts, three years for wattle-and-daub, and five years for brick. A general *ration scale* is established; this endeavours to overcome the difficulty of local scarcity of certain items, by requiring a diet scale composed of certain fixed units, as follows:

Proteins	100 grammes
Carbohydrates . . .	600 ,,
Fats	75 ,,
Fresh fruit or vegetables .	150 ,,
Salt	15 · ,,

An elaborate table is appended, showing the exact values of all ordinary articles of food, to enable the employer to compile his own scale so as to comply with the requirements of the law in a manner best suited to his circumstances.

Ordinance No. 6 of the Katanga Province (Feb. 13, 1930) authorized the proclamation of certain localities in which natives must report their arrival and secure a circulation permit, renewable every seven days.

BRITISH COLONIES, PROTECTORATES, AND MANDATED TERRITORIES

BASUTOLAND

THE law relating to labour consists principally of Proclamation No. 27 of 1907, amended by No. 48 of 1912.

(NOTE. Basutoland being a labour-exporting country, the control and welfare of workers depends mainly on regulations in force outside Basutoland; this accounts for the absence of rules and organization which might otherwise be expected.)

Contract. Six to nine months. Every recruit must be recorded on a written contract attested before an official. Advances are limited to £2, exclusive of rail fare or tax. Contracts executed with the help of a chief or headman are invalid.

Forced Labour. Limited to certain tribal obligations.

Pass Law. Not in force in Basutoland.

Penal Sanctions. In Basutoland a native is liable to a fine of £10 or imprisonment for six months for obtaining an advance from more than one labour agent, or for desertion.

Recruiting. Licensed private labour agents only. The permit is issued by the Resident Commissioner, price £15, while a security of £100 is required from the agent. Recruiters are liable to fines up to £25 or £50, or in default of payment, up to three or six months' imprisonment, for offences such as recruiting without a licence, making false representations, crimping, failing to make the prescribed monthly return, and giving an advance in excess of the permitted amount.

Welfare measures, compensation, and care of women and children are governed by the laws of the countries in which the workers are employed.

Age for contracts is limited to 18 years and over, by Proclamation 48 of 1912.

BRITISH BECHUANALAND

The law relating to labour is based generally on the Cape Masters and Servants Law, amended by Proclamation. The latter consists of: No. 45 of 1907, containing the principal legislation, detailing the licensing of *labour agents*, and regulating *recruiting*; a guarantee of £100 is required from the recruiter, who is liable to a fine of £25 or three months' imprisonment for infringing regulations.

No. 8 of 1925 amends the Cape Masters and Servants Acts of 1856 to 1889, in so far as they apply to Bechuanaland; and 'withholding wages' is altered to 'failure to pay'.

No. 7 of 1909 provides for attestation of *contracts* before a government official, and for *passes* to be produced before an attesting official. No. 10 of 1912 lays down penalties for desertion after contract, or entering into a second contract while one is uncompleted; also limits the amount of *advances* to recruits to £2 exclusive of charges for railway transport or tax. No. 45 of 1919 increases the charge for a labour agent's licence to £25. No. 62 of 1921 amends sections 14 and 17 of No. 7 of 1909, by removing the limitation of claims in respect of which security has to be found by the labour agent.

(NOTE. Bechuanaland being a labour-exporting country, from which men go to work mainly in the Union of South Africa, the control and welfare of workers depends principally on the regulations in force outside the Protectorate; this accounts for the absence of rules and organization which might otherwise be expected.)

Contract. Usual contract is for six months. Mining contracts are generally in number of shirts. All recruits must be taken before an official for the attesting of a written contract. Advances are limited to £2 exclusive of railway charges or tax. A voluntary deferred pay system is reported as working satisfactorily. Recruiting with the help of chiefs renders any contract illegal.

Forced Labour. For tribal purposes, resort may be had to the old tribal system of 'regiments'; if this labour is employed for any government purpose, it must be paid.

Pass Law. There is no registration of natives in the Protectorate, but the labourer is identified by the production of his last tax ticket. Proclamation No. 7 of 1909 requires passes to be prepared by labour agents, for counter-signature by an official.

Penal Sanctions. In the Protectorate a native is liable to a fine of £10 or in default two months' hard labour for (*a*) obtaining an advance from more than one labour agent; and (*b*) desertion after contracting.

Recruiting. Licensed private recruiters only. Permit, price £25, necessary for each agent, and also for each runner, price £1; issued by an authorized officer, subject to the Resident's approval.

The agent before being licensed must obtain the permission of the native chief concerned, and must furnish particulars of the employers for whom he is working. Penalty for non-compliance, £25 or three months' imprisonment.

Wage fixing, machinery, welfare measures, and care of women and children, are governed by the laws of the countries in which the workers are employed.

Proclamation No. 81 of 1921, amended by No. 37 of 1930, gives magistrates wide powers over juveniles up to 18 years of age, 25 years on special certificate, to facilitate their transfer to a reformatory in place of a sentence of imprisonment.

THE GAMBIA

The principal legislation consists of Cap. 67 of the Laws of (Ordinance 38 of 1916) Manual Labour. This applies to 'servants, labourers, and mechanics' excluding Europeans. *Contract* may be by task, or weekly in the case of mechanics and labourers, or monthly in the case of servants. *Penal Sanctions*. Failure to complete contract is punishable with a fine of £2 or in default one month's imprisonment. An employee dismissed before the expiry of the contract may recover up to one month's wages. *Crimping* is punishable with a fine of £10 or in default two months' imprisonment. *Accepting more than one contract* simultaneously is punishable with a fine of £1 or in default fourteen days' imprisonment. The contract is normally for payment in current coin, but may be expressly varied.

Foreign Contracts. The regulations for these will be found to be substantially the same as those of the Nigerian Code (which see). The following are the principal differences. The authorities permitting and approving a foreign contract include in the case of the Gambia, a Travelling Commissioner; the permit to recruit is issued by the Colonial Secretary; particulars of recruiting for foreign contract are to be posted at certain principal places, and notified to chiefs; a capitation fee fixed at £1 per labourer is levied, to be credited to general revenue.

Domestic Servants. Cap. 66 of the Laws (Ordinance 21 of 1922, and 1 of 1925, modified by the Ordinance of September 15, 1931). By this all domestic servants are to be licensed by the Commissioner of Police, for a fee of two shillings; the latter is to maintain a register of domestic servants, fee for search of particulars of servant's record one shilling. Employing an unlicensed servant is punishable with a fine of £20. The employer must give correct particulars of character under penalty of a fine of £10.

Slavery is abolished by Cap. 4 of the Laws (Ordinance 5 of 1906) affirmed by the Ordinance of August 15, 1930.

Forced Labour. Cap. 69 of the Laws (Protectorate Ordinance of 1913) authorizes the Governor in Council to make regulations for the maintenance and construction of roads and bridges; for this purpose chiefs may call upon all able-bodied males in their jurisdiction.

THE GOLD COAST, AND THE MANDATED TERRITORY OF TOGOLAND

The law in the Gold Coast relating to labour is based mainly on Cap. 101 of the Laws (Ordinance 11 of 1921 and 1 of 1924). By this, the definition of 'servant' includes any domestic not under the age of 10 years.

The *Home Contract* (i.e. in the Gold Coast) must be in writing if for longer than six months, and its validity is limited to three years. Written contracts must be attested by the District Commissioner, and must specify the usual particulars of employer and employee, and in addition the nature and place of work and the wages to be paid. These may be in money or kind, but the nature must be specified in the contract. The law covers cases of contract for 'the use of land for tillage' where payment of money for services need not be included. One copy of the contract is retained by the District Officer attesting it, and attested copies may be given to any one desiring them.

Foreign Contracts are limited to thirteen months. They may only be authorized for countries approved by the Secretary of State; recruiters for foreign contracts must be specially authorized by the Governor, and the work must be recommended by the government of the country of employment. All foreign contracts are liable to a charge of one shilling per head, and must be witnessed by the District Commissioner, who shall notify the police at the port of embarkation, and also the Secretary for Native affairs, who shall notify the government of the place of employment. The police must check the rolls on embarkation. The Secretary for Native Affairs may require a bond from the labour agent, to cover wages, repatriation costs and any other expenses.

On expiration of contract, a return passage must be provided within a fortnight, if possible (penalty for delay, a fine of £20 or one month's imprisonment). *Half wages* must be paid on return to the Colony.

The contract is cancelled, and the licence to recruit is withdrawn, on proof of any maltreatment of labourers.

Any District Commissioner or Customs Officer may call upon the master of any ship to muster his crew and passengers for inspection in connexion with these rules.

The Governor is empowered to prohibit recruiting as seems desirable.

Penalty for infringement of conditions of recruiting for foreign contract, £100 and/or two years' imprisonment.

Apprenticeship is regulated; apprentices can be bound with their own consent and that of their guardians, or failing any guardian, that of the District Commissioner; this must be by deed, the age limit being between 9 and 16. No apprentice may be taken out of the Colony. Penalty for crimping an apprentice, a fine of £25 and/or three months' imprisonment.

Breach of Contract. The law originally authorized courts to review and vary terms of contracts, order arrest of absconding defendant in case of breach, and whip offenders under the age of 16; penalty for offences, £20 and/or three month's imprisonment; or for absconding while an advance of wages is owing, up to six month's imprisonment, or for a carrier failing to deliver goods, without reason, one year. These penal clauses were abolished by Ordinance 20 of 1931, which left the enforcement of the contract to the course of law.

Labour Agents. Must be able to produce an authority from the employer whom they serve, on demand by a judge or a District Commissioner. They must have a permit from the Secretary of Mines or a District Commissioner. Recruiting by employers is not covered by these clauses. (Permit introduced by Rule No. 7 of 1921.)

Women. Women are prohibited from night work, except in connexion with certain seasonal industries, or in cases of demonstrable emergency. Penalty for infringement, a fine of £10 and/or imprisonment for one month, per woman employed.

Children. Under 14, may not be employed on any vessel unless in company with their family. Ordinance 22 of 1928, applied to

Ashanti by Note 13 of 1929, established reformatories and regulated the care of juvenile offenders.

Women and Children. By the Mining Regulations, Cap. 107, no woman, and no boy under 14, may be employed underground.

Crimping under any contract is punishable with a fine of £50.

Inspection. Any Police or District Officer may inspect any premises on which labour is employed, to ensure observance of the provisions of the law.

Regulations for the better carrying out of the terms of the law may be made by the Governor in Council.

Other Legislation bearing upon Labour Matters.

Slave Dealing. Abolished by Ordinance 1 of 1874, Cap. 152 of the Laws; emancipation conferred, Ordinance 2 of 1874, Cap. 153 of the Laws. These Ordinances were reaffirmed and enlarged by Ordinance 20 of 1930 (applied to Ashanti by Note 10 of 1930).

Native Administration. Cap. 111 of the Laws. This authorizes 'native customary laws' in so far as these are not opposed to colonial law; details of the extent to which custom might apply to labour are not forthcoming.

Registration of Domestic Servants. Rules No. 25 of 1926, and 5, 14, and 22 of 1927.

All domestic servants of Europeans must be licensed by the Police; the licence must show full personal details and must carry a photograph or finger-prints of the holder. A space is provided on which any employer must enter particulars of service on engagement and discharge, with remarks; the licence is otherwise to remain in the possession of the servant. All fresh employment must be notified to the police within three days, and the licence must be stamped by them accordingly; they will maintain a central register of domestic servants. Penalty for failure to comply with the rules, or for impersonation in connexion with them, a fine of £5.

Mining Health Areas. Cap. 106 of the Laws (Ordinances 19 of 1925, 11 of 1927, and Regulations 19 of 1927). This empowers the Governor to make regulations for the housing, feeding, sanitation, and medical care, of labourers in mining areas; also for the reporting of sickness or death. Penalty for non-compliance with rules, a fine of £100 and/or imprisonment for one year. Cap. 107 of the Laws gives detailed requirements to ensure safety of working of mines, and authorizes the appointment of inspectors.

Forced Labour. The Roads Ordinance, Cap. 107 of the Laws, amended by Ordinance 9 of 1924, authorizes Provincial Commissioners to require native authorities to maintain roads passing through their districts, all able-bodied males being liable up to twenty-four days in one year. Penalty for non-compliance, a fine of £1 or imprisonment for one month. Payment for such work is made by the District Commissioner, after inspection, to the chief, at the rate of five shillings to one pound for non-motorable roads, or two pounds to ten pounds for motorable roads, per mile completed.

KENYA

The principal legislation relating to labour in Kenya is contained in the Employment of Natives Law (Cap. 139 of the Laws of Kenya, embodying seven ordinances dating from 1910 to 1920 reaffirmed by Ordinance 21 of 1927). The following is a summary of the provisions.

Foreign Contracts must be in writing and must receive the approval of the Governor; a bond may be required. Penalty for decoying servants abroad, £100 fine, or one year's imprisonment.

Local Contracts. These must be written, if the engagement is for more than one month, and attested by magistrate or Justice of the Peace; they must specify the name and particulars of the servant, with the place, nature, and duration of the work, and the rate of wage, which must be paid not less often than monthly. Three copies are made, one for the employer, one for the headman, and an original for deposition in the administrative office of the district of recruitment.

Validity of Contract. A limit of two years.

Crimping is prohibited under penalty of a fine of £5 or six months' imprisonment.

Apprenticeship is sanctioned in the case of boys between the ages of 9 and 14, at the desire of the father, and with the consent of the child.

Care of Servants. They must be 'properly' housed and fed; blankets must be supplied on demand, to be paid for by the servant. Tents must be provided for journeys with porters. Medical care must be furnished, and food must be given for the return journey after completion of contract. Labour Inspectors are maintained, for supervisory purposes, under the direction of the Medical Department.

Courts. Cases under the Employment of Natives Law must be tried by first or second-class courts, and either criminal or civil procedure may be followed. The magistrate has power to vary the terms of the contract. Juveniles may be punished by whipping with a light cane in place of imprisonment.

Penal Sanctions. Minor Offences by Servants. Failing to start work when contracted; absence; drunkenness; carelessness in carrying out work; using vehicle without permission; use of insulting or abusive language; refusal to obey a lawful order; giving of a false name or particulars in contract. Penalty, fine of £5 and/or imprisonment for one month.

Major Offences by Servants. Causing damage by neglect or carelessness; neglect of proper precautions for safety of property; cattle herd failing to report death of stock; deceptively describing loss of property; desertion with intention not to return. Penalty £7 10s. 0d. fine and/or six months' imprisonment. Cognizable offence, and police may arrest without warrant. The employer may be compensated by order of the court, for lost property.

Offences by Employers. 'Withholding' wages; detaining property of servant; failing to supply food, shelter, or other necessaries specified by law. Penalty, £10 fine and/or one month's imprisonment.

The Governor is empowered to appoint special magistrates and labour inspectors.

Medical Officers are empowered to make inspections, and condemn food or accommodation, vary the ration given, require the necessary stock of drugs to be maintained, order blankets to be provided, or send employees to hospital when necessary.

Medical Inspection of Recruits. Compulsory for labour agents; the examination is free. The employment of boys under 16 is prohibited in the case of certain types of work, such as porterage, ricksha pulling, &c.

Labour Agents. (Rules under the Ordinance of April 4, 1910.) Permits must be obtained from Senior Commissioners, and are terminable yearly. They must specify the places of recruitment and of employment; a fee of ten shillings must be paid, and a bond may be required. Labour agents must have written authorization from employers for whom they are working, and must notify the District Commissioner of their arrival when recruiting. They must supply food to their recruits for the journey.

Labourers' Diet. (Rule of August 17, 1921, based on Ordinance.)

A special diet scale is laid down, giving alternatives in carbo-hydrates, proteins, fats, and vitamins; also 2 oz. of salt, and half a lemon four days a week. This scale applies only to workers in railway fuel camps. (Some valuable research work on tribal diets has been carried out by the Medical Department.[1])

Women Workers. (Rule of March 20, 1923, based on the Ordinance.) Employers of women may not allow them to remain at the place of employment for the night unless accompanied by their husbands or fathers; penalty for each infringement, fine of fifty shillings.

Medical Treatment. (Government Notice under the Ordinance, No. 375 of 1926.) Medical treatment must be provided; a supply of certain drugs (according to schedule given) must be maintained; the employer is liable to hospital maintenance of the servant for thirty days or till the end of the contract, if shorter, for all but casual labourers.

Other Laws having some bearing on Labour Matters.

Liquor Ordinance. (Cap. 71 of the Laws.) Refers to European liquor. No native may be employed to sell this, under penalty of £75 fine, or three months' imprisonment. No native may be supplied with liquor; penalty, first offence, £150 fine or six months' imprisonment, up to penalty for third offence, minimum, imprisonment for two years, with fine up to £1,200.

Native Liquor Ordinance. (Ordinance 20 of 1921. Cap. 133 of the Laws and Ordinances 36 of 1930.) Sales to be on specified licensed premises; no women are to be employed on licensed premises without special permission. Proceeds of licences to be expended on native welfare.

Native Registration. (Ordinance 56 of 1921, Cap. 127 of the Laws.) Every adult male native is to carry a registration certificate of specified form (the application of the Ordinance is by rule, as requisite; the effect appears to be to apply the provisions generally to natives outside the reserves); any employer must endorse the certificate within twenty-four hours of engagement and on dis-charge, and he must keep a register of employees. Penalty for omission, £30 fine or three months' imprisonment.

The form of the registration certificate is prescribed by rule:

[1] 'Studies of Nutrition, Physique and Health among two African Tribes.' Orr and Gilks, 1931. H.M's Stationery Office.

requirements are; name, father, district, tribe, location, subloca-
tion, group, clan, circumcision age, date, signature of official
issuing. Blank space for signatures by employers, details of
wages, &c. Finger-prints of all ten fingers; index letters and
numbers. A metal container is provided free; fee for replacing
lost certificate, two shillings; fee for replacing lost container, one
shilling.

Offences by natives with reference to certificates. Using another
man's certificate, mutilating, altering, or refusing to produce a
certificate, or duplicate registration. Penalty, £15 fine and/or
three months' imprisonment.

Offences in Connexion with Certificates. Withholding; failing to
enter engagement or discharge; destroying or tampering with
certificate; employing any unregistered native. Penalty, £100 fine
and/or one year's imprisonment.

Finger prints are made admissible evidence; a central finger-
print bureau is established.

Native Exemption. (Cap. 128 of the Laws.) Educated natives
may be granted letters of exemption on application to the Chief
Native Commissioner, which relieve them of registration requirements. The letter must be carried and produced when required
by any magistrate, police officer, or any employer when on his
property. Deposit on application, £4, repayable; fee, two shillings;
valid for one year. Penalty for any infringement, thirty shillings
fine or in default, seven days' simple imprisonment. Schedule
consists of ordained priests or ministers, barristers, qualified
doctors, dentists, chemists, or engineers.

Under Ordinance 56, the Rules in Government Notice 375 of
1926 gave certain details relating to the renewal of the certificate.
Government Notice 12 of 1927 applied the main Ordinance to
casual labour and ricksha boys. Government Notice 549 of 1928
gave certain details relating to the taking of finger-prints.

Native Authority. (Cap. 129 of the Laws, covering five Ordinances from 1912 to 1922.) This authorized headmen to require
six days' work a quarter, from all able-bodied males, on water-
courses or other work for the benefit of the community to which the
workers belong. There is no mention of payment for this work.

Headmen are also authorized to require paid labour for urgent
repairs to roads, railways, or government works, or to deal with
fire, flood, or other emergency.

Headmen may requisition paid porters for transport of officers' baggage and stores urgently required.

Labour may also be requisitioned, at local rates of pay, for work on roads, railways, and other government undertakings, certified in each case as being of public benefit by the Governor, after previous approval by the Secretary of State.

Exemption is granted on proof of three months' work during the previous twelve months, or for other occupation already accepted. Limit, sixty days per annum; penalty for non-compliance, a fine of £7 10s. 0d. or two months' imprisonment.

Roads Ordinance. (Cap. 114, Ordinance 12 of 1912.) Under this Ordinance, chiefs may call upon able-bodied males for six days' labour per quarter on roads or bridges within their jurisdiction. Payment not mentioned. Penalty for non-compliance, fine of thirty shillings or one month's imprisonment.

Credit Trade with Natives. (Cap. 130 of the Laws.) Debts from natives of over £10 cannot be legally recovered unless the transaction was attested by the District Commissioner.

Resident Natives Ordinance. (This was originally Ordinance 33 of 1918, Cap. 132 of the Laws. This was revived by Ordinance 19 of 1924, as a result of the disallowance by His Majesty of the Masters and Servants Amendment Ordinance of 1924. These Ordinances were repealed and replaced by the Resident Native Labourers Ordinance, No. 5 of 1925.) This authorizes a contract by the head of any family with the occupier of any land, whereby the family is permitted to reside on the land in return for 180 days' labour per annum by the head and any male member of the family, for wages. The contract may be for one to three years, and must be made in writing, before a magistrate, and must specify the rate of wages, and provide for the supply of building material for huts, use of grazing land, &c. It is terminable on six months' notice on either side, the family having a right to their crops or compensation in lieu, in case of disturbance. The magistrate may refuse to approve any contract in which he considers the wages to be fixed at an unfair figure. Natives may only reside on farms under the terms of this Ordinance, and may only move to a farm with the approval of their District Commissioner certified on a permit from the magistrate of the district where the farm is situated. The occupier must keep a register showing the number of days worked by each tenant, and the wages paid, also a register of all cattle kept by the tenants. Payments in cash by the tenants are prohibited.

Minor Offences by Natives. Failure to begin duties; absence from work; drunkenness; neglect or carelessness in work; using a vehicle without permission; abusive language to the employer; refusal to obey a lawful order; penalty, fine of £5 and/or one month's imprisonment.

Major Offences by Servants. Damage caused through drunkenness; risk to property through drunkenness or neglect; when employed as herdsman, failing to report death or loss of animal in his care; neglectful loss of property. Penalty, fine of £7 10s. 0d. and/or two months' imprisonment.

Offences by Employers. Withholding wages; detaining property of a servant. Penalty, fine of £10 and/or one month's imprisonment. (NOTE: Rules, with forms of registers to be employed, appeared on July 3, 1925, and October 12, 1925.)

The Native Authority Amendment Ordinance, No. 16 of 1928, authorizes a Provincial or District Commissioner to order back to his reserve any native cultivating elsewhere without permission, the native being one of a tribe for whom reserves have been provided.

Registration of Domestic Servants Ordinance. (No. 11 of 1929, and 46 of 1931.) The provisions of this Ordinance have to be 'applied' as required, to townships, &c., by Government Notice.

Registrars have to be appointed; every servant must be registered and must receive a pocket register, in which the employer must enter all particulars of employment on engagement and discharge, the register being retained by the employer during employment. The register must show particulars of the servant, and must also include photograph or finger-prints of the holder; no servant may be engaged without one.

Offences by Employers. Omission of any of the foregoing requirements, and the entry of unjustifiable adverse remarks as to character; penalty a fine of £5.

Offences by Servants. Non-compliance with the requirements of the Ordinance, a fine of £2 10s. 0d. and/or three months' imprisonment; giving a false name or particulars in connexion with registration, a fine of £5 and/or six months' imprisonment.

General Offences. Destroying any register; counterfeiting any part of one; making any false entry; making false certified copy. Penalty, a fine of £10 and/or one year's imprisonment. The taking of finger-prints in this connexion is authorized. The Governor is authorized to make rules for the better carrying out of the law.

(NOTE. The rules published in Government Notice 497 of 1930 give additional details regarding the use of finger-prints or photographs; specify the method of entering a record of any conviction for a criminal offence; and provide for the return of lost pocket registers.)

The Vagrancy Ordinance. Cap. 63 of the Laws. (Ordinances 9 of 1920, 32 of 1921, and 21 of 1930.) This applies to any person without visible means of support. Police may arrest without warrant. A magistrate may order a vagrant to find work, to return to his tribal reserve, or to be detained in a house of detention. The Superintendent of the House of Detention shall seek suitable work for the vagrant, who must accept it under penalty of six months' imprisonment for failing to do so. Vagrants under 16 years of age may be handed over to their guardians, or punished with six strokes of the cane. The Governor is authorized to establish houses of detention, with Superintendents and Medical Officers to take charge of them.

The Shop Hours Ordinance. (No. 24 of 1925 and 40 of 1930.) This makes provision for a weekly half-holiday, Sunday closing, meal hours, a fifty-hour week or a nine-hour day; also for annual leave, and seating accommodation for female attendants. There is no colour distinction in the Ordinance. Penalty for infringement, fine of £5 or fourteen days' simple imprisonment up to a fine of £30 or two months' simple imprisonment for a third offence. The police may supervise the observation of this Ordinance.

Detention Camps Ordinance. (No. 25 of 1925.) This creates detention camps, to which offenders may be sent as an alternative to prison, in the case of certain scheduled Ordinances which include the Masters and Servants, Vagrancy, and Resident Native Labourers Ordinances. The Governor in Council is authorized to make rules for the management and discipline of these camps.

NIGERIA, AND THE MANDATED TERRITORY OF THE CAMEROONS

Earlier legislation on labour was repealed by the Labour Code, Ordinance No. 1 of 1929, which replaced all previous laws. Among the definitions are 'Assisted Emigrant', which means a labourer on foreign contract; 'Government contract service', which recognizes special government labour contracts; 'Labourer', which means any unskilled labourer paid less than four shillings per diem; and 'Labour health areas', which may be proclaimed as such by the Governor. (For particulars of these, see *infra*.)

Contracts. These must be in writing for periods over six months. They are valid for a limit of two years. They must specify nature and place of work, pay, and date of payment, in addition to the usual particulars of master and servant, and must be attested by a magistrate. Three copies are made, one for record in the magistrate's office, and one each for the employer and the employee. Wages must be paid in money, though part payment in food is sanctioned.

'Tillage contracts' involving no money payments, are recognized.

Penalty. Any employer paying wages in kind, failing to supply the stipulated food, housing, or medical comforts, or 'withholding' wages, may be sentenced for a first offence £10, and for a third offence £25 and/or imprisonment for two months.

Crimping is punishable with a fine of £10.

Foreign Contracts may only be made for employment in countries approved by the Secretary of State; no native may accept one without the sanction of an administrative officer (penalty, a fine of £25 and/or three months' imprisonment). The administrative officer must satisfy himself that the native is fit to work, is over the age of 16, is not abandoning any dependent relatives, and is not absconding to avoid liability under native law.

Agents for Foreign Contracts must be licensed by the Governor, for periods not exceeding three months, and for a specified number of recruits, and only on recommendation from the government of the country of employment. All such permits are to be notified to other British West African colonies. Except for government service, the Governor shall require security for wages and expenses of recruits. Contracts must be made before a magistrate, who shall endorse on the permit the number of men recruited; a copy of the contract is to be sent to the government recommending the agent. Another copy is to be sent to the police at the port of embarkation, who must check the muster roll on embarkation. The magistrate is to keep a register of men absent on foreign contract. The fees for foreign contracts are fixed by the Governor in Council. Masters of ships must satisfy themselves that passengers are not infringing the above provisions; they must furnish a list of deck passengers to the Police or Customs Officers; they may be required to muster their deck passengers for inspection; and in a foreign port they may only discharge deck passengers from Nigeria before a British Consul. Penalty for infringement, a fine of £20 or in default three months' imprisonment.

Duration of Foreign Contracts, thirteen months. On expiry, a return passage must be arranged, if possible, within a fortnight; penalty for non-compliance, a fine of £20 or in default one month's imprisonment. Half wages must be paid in Nigeria.

Misconduct on the part of employer or agent cancels the contract without prejudice to the labourer's rights thereunder.

Penalty for fraudulent recruiting for foreign service, a fine of £100 and/or two years' imprisonment.

Breach of Contract. Triable by the ordinary courts. An absconding defendant may be arrested, and the courts may adjust the terms of a contract, and award fines for breach up to £20, and in aggravated cases, up to one month's imprisonment; offenders under 16 years of age may be punished with twelve strokes.

The Governor in Council may make regulations for porterage, apprenticeship, identification, repatriation, medical examination, housing, rations, planning, and lay-out of 'labour health areas', care of sick and injured, licensing and registration of domestics, and for 'imposing upon persons who have accepted the services of a servant without paying wages therefor, the obligation to provide for the maintenance of such servant during sickness or old age'. Also the appointment of a Labour Inspector and officers; and workmen's compensation for injury.

Regulation No. 172 of 1929, under the Labour Code, declares thirty areas in the Cameroons 'labour health areas'. (NOTE: these consist of plantations, &c.)

'Labour Health Areas.' (Regulation No. 6 of 1929.) For these, full regulations are made for housing, water, sanitation, &c. Permits for buildings for more than twenty-five men must be obtained previously from an administrative officer. Details may be modified with the approval of the Director of Medical Services. Drainage and latrine arrangements must satisfy the Government Medical Officer. A hospital must be provided if there is no government one available; a scale of equipment is laid down, and this must satisfy the Director of Medical Services. If the number of employees reaches 5,000, a special medical officer must be

employed. Every labour health area and each hospital in it must be visited by a medical officer at intervals laid down according to scale of importance. All building plans must be approved by an administrative officer. Employers must furnish lists showing details of the numbers employed, and a monthly return of deaths must be rendered to the administrative officer.

Regulation No. 6 of 1929 regulates the *method of payment*, which must be weekly or monthly, and secures a *weekly day of rest*, unless for exceptional circumstances. The employer must give the servant an *attendance book* (according to the schedule attached) and must mark this daily with the record of attendance, entering all wages paid; a magistrate may demand the production of this book, and may check deductions from wages. The expiry of the contract ends any claim for advance of wages. *Housing, food, and medical resources* must satisfy the administrative or medical officer. A scale of rations is laid down, for use if these are issued; it consists of a weekly issue on the following scale: 12 lb. of rice, 2 lb. of beans or ground-nuts, and 6 oz. of salt (or 2 oz. with 2 lb. of green food). This may be varied, but the 'nutritive value' must not be less. Medical officers may issue 'reasonable directions' as to rations supplied.

A ten-hour day is introduced.

Repatriation expenses are secured for the employees.

Death or injury must be reported to the nearest magistrate.

Compensation is introduced; this may amount to £25 for death, £20 for total incapacity, and £10 for partial incapacity; serious or wilful misconduct excludes compensation. The amount of the compensation is fixed by a magistrate, but any civil liability is also recognized.

Accidents render the employer liable for hospital expenses.

Inspection of premises by administrative or medical officer, or inspectors of labour, is authorized.

Carriers' loads are limited to sixty-five pounds; if sick, they must be provided for.

Penalty for infringement of any of the above rules: for a first offence, a fine of £10, and subsequently up to a fine of £50 or imprisonment for six months.

Women and Children. By the Labour Code (Ordinance 1 of 1929) night work is prohibited for women, except in emergency or in connexion with certain products; penalty, a fine of £10 or one month's imprisonment for each woman so employed. No *children* under 16 may be employed underground, or on machine work.

Apprenticeship is provided for by the Labour Code between the ages of 9 and 16; the consent of the apprentice and that of his guardian are necessary, but if no guardian is available, the Lieut.-Governor may act instead. Such agreements must be in writing, and must be completed before a magistrate. *Crimping* of an apprentice is punishable with a fine of £50 and/or six months' imprisonment.

Orphans or delinquent juveniles are provided for by Cap. 82 of the Laws, amended by Ordinance 35 of 1928, which enables a magistrate to consign them to the care of a suitable person or establishment, when under the age of 15, to remain there until eighteen.

Slavery. Legal status abolished by Cap. 83 of the Laws. (Ordinances 35 of 1916, and 20 of 1918.)

Forced Labour. The Native Authority Law, Cap. 73 of the Laws, empowers native authorities to issue orders to natives 'for any other purpose approved by the Governor'. In the Mandated Territory of the Cameroons 'the only form in which forced labour is exacted for the Government is for the transport of loads for government officials on tour and of essential stores'. This labour is paid at the current rate. (Report on the Administration of the British Cameroons, 1925.) In the native administrations, maintenance of roads other than main roads is carried on without payment, new construction being paid for. (Ibid.) The former use of unpaid compulsory labour on roads and rivers in Nigeria ceased under the terms of Ordinance 18 of 1927, which repealed Cap. 107 of the Laws.

NYASALAND

The law relating to labour in Nyasaland is based mainly on the Employment of Natives Ordinance of 1909, as amended by Ordinance 14 of 1911, and No. 13 of 1926; and the District Administration (Native) Ordinance of 1924.

The *Contract* may be oral up to one month, but must be in writing for longer periods. Ordinance 26 of 1929 introduced a twenty-six working days' contract, to be completed in forty-two days.

Wages must be in cash; penalty for withholding wages, first offence, fine of £5 or one month's imprisonment; up to a third offence, for which the penalty is a fine of £50 or six months' imprisonment. Ordinance 13 of 1926 made wages a prior claim on employers' property.

Employing without means of payment is punishable with a fine of £100 or imprisonment for one year.

Welfare. Provision for housing, feeding, and medical attention are to be inserted in the contract. Penalty for non-compliance with these, fine of £25 or three months' imprisonment. Provisions were elaborated by Ordinance 7 of 1929.

Crimping is punishable with a fine of £25 or three months' imprisonment.

Penal Sanctions. Employers are liable to the above penalties for failure to comply with requirements regarding wages, food, housing, and medical attention. For employees, there is no division into major and minor offences, as in the East African codes. Offences are: giving false name on engagement; desertion; drunkenness; neglect of duty. Penalty: first conviction, fine of three shillings or one month's imprisonment; second conviction: fine of nine shillings or three months' imprisonment.

A Pass Law applies to natives leaving the Protectorate.

Recruiting. For employment outside the Protectorate a Governor's licence is necessary, and powers to regulate this are conferred.

Other Legislation bearing upon Labour Matters.

The new Penal Code, introduced by Ordinance 22 of 1929, made it an offence to produce any *fraudulent written character* when applying for employment; penalty, one year's imprisonment.

Natives on Private Estates. (Ordinance 15 of 1928.) This is a squatter law. Payment may be in cash or in work; compensation must be given for disturbance; six months' notice to quit must be given; registration of residence is compulsory; an offending tenant may be ejected by order of the District Commissioner; measures for regulating the growth of economic crops are authorized.

Credit to Natives. Ordinance 5 of 1903, amplified by Ordinance 15 of 1926, makes any advance to natives legally irrecoverable unless previously approved by the Resident.

Forced Labour. Ordinance 11 of 1924, District Administration, sanctioned compulsory work for able-bodied adult males, at the current rate of wages, on gazetted public works (on Governor's previous recommendation, approved by the Secretary of State); this is limited to sixty days per annum, and two months' previous work on contract confers exemption. District Residents may give orders for compulsory employment as porters, or for work for the benefit of the village, or in emergencies. Headmen failing to perform their duties under this section are liable to a fine of £5 or three months' imprisonment; natives refusing to carry out such orders are liable to a fine of £1 or one month's imprisonment.

RHODESIA (NORTHERN)

The law relating to labour was brought up to date by the Employment of Natives Ordinance, No. 56 of 1929.

(NOTE. Northern Rhodesia was formerly mainly a labour-exporting country; recent mining development has increased the local demand for labour, which will in future probably be attracted into the country.)

The principal provisions of the Ordinance are as follows:

Contract. Oral, up to thirty days; written, up to two years. Three copies of the written contract are required, for the employer, the servant, and for filing in the administrative office where the contract has been confirmed by a magistrate.

Housing, feeding, and medical attention must be provided by the employer, unless other arrangements are made for food. Servants are entitled to one month's full pay as a maximum when sick.

(NOTE. Ord. 12 of 1930 confers wide general powers of inspection and control of insanitary premises, food, &c.)

Repatriation expenses and food must be provided by the employer. Inspection is authorized by medical and administrative officers.

(NOTE. Ordinance 41 of 1930 makes provision for a Labour Commissioner and officers to give special attention to labour matters.)

Cash payment of wages is obligatory.

Recruiters are licensed by the Secretary for Native Affairs. Bond (amount fixed by Governor) at present £100 for Rhodesia, or £250 for foreign contracts. Licence must specify district of recruitment, and employers served; runners must be licensed and must wear badges. Recruiting must be on contract, and is prohibited on private property. 'Labour Districts' in which recruiting is prohibited, may be gazetted under Ordinance 41 of 1930.

Medical inspection of contract labourers is compulsory, at a fee fixed by the Governor.

Foreign Contracts must be specially prepared, for work outside Rhodesia; penalty for enticing a native without contract, £100 fine or one year's imprisonment.

Recruiting through chiefs, or *crimping*, is punishable with a fine of £50 or six months' imprisonment.

Penal Sanctions. Offences by Employers. Withholding wages; detaining employee's property; failure to supply food when this is in the contract; non-compliance with regulations for safety or welfare. Penalty, fine of £50, and/or three months' imprisonment.

Offences by Employee. Minor. Desertion, drunkenness, damage caused through neglect, abusive language, refusal to work, giving a wrong name, brawling. Penalty, fine of half-month's wages, or one month's imprisonment.

Major Offences. Damage or risk caused through drunkenness; failure to maintain safety regulations; neglect of animals; loss of property through neglect; desertion with intent not to return. Penalty, fine of £10 or six months' imprisonment.

Breach of Contract. Ordinance No. 8 of 1929 sanctions arrest of deserters without warrant.

Whipping may be administered to juveniles in place of imprisonment at the discretion of the courts.

Offences under the Ordinance are triable by the ordinary courts, and civil procedure may be used at discretion.

Children and married women can only be contracted with the consent of their guardian. Juveniles under 14 must have a certificate from the Secretary for Native Affairs (Ordinance 10 of 1926).

Apprenticeship for five years is sanctioned, the District Officer being the guardian.

Compensation for accidents may be awarded by the courts up to two years' wages. Ordinance No. 16 of 1930 introduces a measure of compensation for disease according to schedule (mainly referring to diseases connected with mining).

Other Legislation bearing on Labour Matters.

Native Pass Ordinances. No. 10 of 1902, amended by 12 of 1904, 6 of 1905, 8 of 1906, 15 of 1913, and 5 of 1922, and further elaborated by the *Registration of Natives Ordinance*, No. 50 of 1929. Every native male over the age of 14 must be registered; identity certificate is issued, giving full particulars, with fingerprints. Every employer must endorse the certificate on employing a workman, and must keep a register of employees; penalty for failing to do so, a fine of £5. Damaging or altering or withholding a certificate by an employer renders him liable to a fine of £50, or on second conviction, three months' imprisonment. Certificates may be demanded by administrative officers, justices of the peace, and police registration officers. Offences by natives are punishable with a fine of £10 or three months' imprisonment.

Natives on Private Estates. (Ordinance No. 57 of 1919.) Landlord must keep a register of these; rent is payable only in service, not in money or kind; sharing of crops is prohibited; an agreement must be concluded before the District Officer.

Credit to Natives. (Ordinance No. 1 of 1912.) Credit may only be legally given to natives with the consent of the District Officer.

Box System. (Ordinance No. 5 of 1915.) This deals with boxes kept for safe custody or security of payment. The keeper must be registered and must hold a general dealer's licence; he must also keep a list of depositors. Penalty for non-compliance, a fine of £25 or three months' imprisonment.

Forced Labour. Ordinance No. 32 of 1929 authorized the calling out of able-bodied males for work on essential public services on certificate by a Provincial Commissioner, for sixty days per annum as a maximum, wages being paid at the current local rate. This is applicable to maintenance of village roads, or when dealing with disease, fire, or other emergencies, or for the planting of food if famine threatens. Penalty for failing to obey such an order, fine of £5 and/or three months' imprisonment.

Native Liquor. Ordinance No. 11 of 1930 regulates the sale of native liquor, which must not contain more than 4 per cent. of alcohol. It may only be sold on licensed premises. Penalty, fine of £10 or three months' imprisonment, or for a subsequent offence, fine of £25 or six months' imprisonment.

RHODESIA (SOUTHERN)

Legislation was originally founded on earlier South African law, but this has gradually been replaced by local ordinances. The principal one is the Masters and Servants Ordinance, No. 5 of 1901, amended by No. 8 of 1929. The following are the main provisions:

Contract. May be oral (one year) or written (three years). In the latter case it must show particulars of master and servant, and

also the date, the length of contract, and the wage. Sickness entitles
the servant to one month's wages while incapacitated. Women
require the consent of their husbands to any contract, and children
under 16 must obtain the consent of their guardians.

Apprenticeship. This is legalized, and must be carried out before
a magistrate; it applies to natives under 16, who must have the
approval of their guardians. Destitute juveniles may be apprenticed
by a magistrate, if no guardian can be found, in which case the wages
must be paid to the credit of the apprentice, and into an account
kept by the magistrate. If the master should move more than four
miles from his original habitation, the deed becomes invalid automatically unless re-approved. Penalties for an apprentice are
established for absence, drunkenness, carelessness in work, wrong-
ful use of vehicle, refusal to obey a lawful order, brawling, abuse of
any headman, loss of property through neglect, failure to report
death or loss of any animal of which he has charge. Punishment,
fine of £4 or in default one month's imprisonment, second offence,
fine of £8 and/or two months' imprisonment. A master who with-
holds wages is liable to a fine of £5 or in default one month's
imprisonment; and for detaining a child under 16 employed as a
domestic servant, or for detaining animals the property of an
apprentice, he is liable to a fine of £10 or in default one month's
imprisonment.

General Penalties. Crimping, or intimidating any servant in
order to prevent his freedom of labour, a fine of £20 and/or
imprisonment for three months.

The right of free discussion of conditions of work is safeguarded.
The Native Juveniles Act, No. 10 of 1926 (brought into operation
by Proclamation 9 of 1927) applies to natives under 14. These
must, when seeking work, have a pass from a Native Commissioner
to certify that they have their guardian's consent. The Native
Commissioner may supervise the conditions of employment, order
the juvenile to return home, or hear any complaint, and may fine
the juvenile up to ten shillings, or order him to receive ten strokes
with a cane (in which case a report of the award and the circumstances must be forwarded to the Attorney-General). Vagrant
juveniles may be contracted to suitable employers up to six months
by Native Commissioners (all such contracts must be reported to
the Chief Native Commissioner). The employment of any juvenile
not in possession of a certificate is punishable with a fine of £10

or in default fourteen days' imprisonment. Employers of juveniles must enter on their certificates the details of the terms of work, and report these to a Native Commissioner within ten days, under same penalty. Juveniles disobeying the orders of a Native Commissioner may be punished with ten strokes of the cane.

Native Labour Regulations. Ordinance No. 16 of 1911 (slightly amended by Ordinances of 1924 and 1927). This establishes licences for labour agents, compound managers, and conductors; recruiting by special companies is authorized; employers must have a licence, but not for recruiting at their place of business. Labour agents' fees; for recruiting for employment in Southern Rhodesia, £1 and a bond of £100; for employment elsewhere, £50 and a bond for £250, bonds expiring six months after the licence; districts of recruitment and employers served must be specified on the licence. Runners must be approved by a magistrate, fee one shilling, and must wear a badge or uniform. Any offence by an agent leads to suspension of his licence, which may be cancelled by the Administrator.

Contracts. All licensees must recruit on contract before a magistrate, who shall explain the purport of the contract to any illiterate employee. *Foreign Contracts* must be stamped to the value of five shillings per month of the contract.

The following *offences* are punishable with a fine of £50 and/or six months' imprisonment: recruiting through chiefs; misrepresenting the conditions of employment; crimping; concealment of a contract-breaker; recruiting on private property.

Offences by natives are: failing to begin work after engagement; causing injury by neglect to persons or property; accepting advance of wages from two different employers. Penalty, a fine of £10 and/or two months' imprisonment.

Withholding wages is punishable with a fine of £50 and/or six months' imprisonment.

(NOTE. Ordinances 1 of 1915 and 6 of 1922 substituted 'failing to pay' for 'Withholding'.)

Compound managers must be appointed by employers of three hundred natives or more.

Inspectors of native labourers may be appointed by the Administrator; their duties are to inquire into grievances, breaches of discipline, or disputes between natives, and to arrest offenders against the law. They can issue summonses, administer oaths, and fine labourers up to £5 from their wages; records of such fines must be sent to a magistrate, to whom an appeal lies. Employers must afford all facilities to Inspectors, under penalty of a fine of £50, or in default six months' imprisonment. The Administrator is authorized to make regulations on numerous subjects, including enforcement or cancellation of contracts, amount of advances, importation of labourers, repatriation, transport conditions, medical examination, housing, food, and sanitation, duties of compound managers, the keeping of particulars of labour, and recruiting.

The Importation of Labourers Ordinance, No. 18 of 1901, establishes a Protector of Immigrants, with Inspectors and Medical Officers. With the Administrator's authorization, the Protector may make rules concerning the welfare of employees. A Sunday rest is established, with a nine-hour working day; wages are to be paid weekly in cash, and the employer must issue a pay-book. Repatriation is secured, and medical inspection on arrival in the country. An Inspector or Medical Officer may inspect all premises where labourers are housed or employed. All deserters must be reported, and the police may arrest them without warrant.

Penalties. Employers failing to keep a register of labourers, or to report deserters, or withholding wages, are liable to a fine of £5 and/or two months' imprisonment; for assaulting an employee they are liable to a fine of £10 and/or three months' imprisonment.

Immigrant labourers are liable to various penalties up to a fine of £10 and/or three months' imprisonment for: altering a pass; refusing to clean a dirty dwelling; drunkenness; refusal to work; or attempting to leave Southern Rhodesia without a pass.

A Native Labour Bureau was established by Ordinance No. 8 of 1911, to replace a former one. This is to be self-supporting but not profit-earning; its objects, *inter alia*, are to procure labour for members, supervise conditions of employment, and facilitate travelling of labourers. The articles of association regulate the subscription; a complement of labour is to be fixed for each member, and labourers are to be shared among members as far as possible; employees wishing to return to previous employers are to be sent to them when feasible.

Forced Labour. The Native Affairs Ordinance, No. 14 of 1927, requires all natives, in addition to giving service in emergencies, to obey 'any lawful or reasonable order' by 'headman, chief, or

Native Commissioner'; this must be 'in conformity with native law or custom' or for the 'general advancement of welfare' of, natives. Penalty for non-compliance, fine of £10 or three months' imprisonment.

Compensation for native labourers in cases of death or injury. Ordinance No. 15 of 1922, amended by Law 16 of 1930, renders the employer liable for compensation to any injured native on the following scale; permanent partial incapacity, £2 to £15; permanent total incapacity, £15 to £50; death, £20. The payments are to be supervised by a Native Commissioner.

(NOTE. The Workmen's Compensation Ordinances 20 of 1922 and 17 of 1930 do not apply to natives.)

The *Shop Hours* Ordinance, No. 12 of 1921, establishes a Sunday rest, regulates hours of employment, and introduces a 47½-hour week.

The *Conciliation Boards* Ordinance, No. 18 of 1920, authorizes the appointment of these by the Administrator; they are to inquire into and deal with disputes between employers and employees; both sides are to be represented, together with a proportion of disinterested members.

Other Legislation affecting Labour Matters.

Registration of Natives. (Ordinances 16 of 1901, 15 of 1913, 10 of 1914, and 3 of 1915, also Native Pass Ordinances Nos. 10 of 1902, and 8 of 1906.) Every male native over 14 must be in possession of a pass, to be obtained from a Pass Officer; when entering on any contract to work, he must in addition obtain a certificate from the Registrar of Natives, who is to see that the terms of the contract are fully understood by the native. The employer must pay one shilling for the certificate, on which he must endorse all the particulars of the employment; the certificate is then given to the native, the pass being retained by the employer. At the termination of the contract, the employer must write a discharge and no further employment is legal without this.

Railway tickets will only be issued to natives on production of a pass.

A *curfew* rule requires all natives in townships to be within doors between the hours of 9 p.m. and 5 a.m. unless with special sanction.

Penalties for employers which vary, and may amount to a fine of £50 and/or six months' imprisonment, are provided for; withholding, destroying, tampering with, or forging, a pass or certificate;

deducting any unauthorized sum from wages; employing a native without a certificate; refusing to certify discharge; making any entry on a certificate except in connexion with a labour contract; fraudulent contract; or crimping.

Penalties for natives to the extent of a fine of £10 and/or three months' imprisonment may be inflicted for: using another's pass or certificate; making a false statement in connexion with the issue of these; failing to produce a pass or certificate; mutilating or altering them. Counterfeiting passes is punishable with six months', or in case of repeated offences, one year's imprisonment.

The Administrator is authorized to make regulations for more effective application, and may regulate fees payable, and the method of taking finger-prints if necessary.

Medical inspection and vaccination is provided for in townships in connexion with passes, by Ordinance 5 of 1918.

The *Private Locations* Ordinance, No. 14 of 1908, authorizes landholders to establish locations on their properties, after application to the Administrator for sanction; the number of natives allowed to reside in these locations is limited, and the landholder is liable for a tax of one shilling per head.

The *Box System* Ordinance, No. 9 of 1912, refers to persons who undertake the custody of boxes the property of native workmen. These persons must be licensed, and must keep a register of all such boxes held by them, which is to be open to inspection. No box may be disposed of without sanction from a magistrate, who may authorize the sale of those unclaimed for six months. Should any box-keeper become bankrupt, the boxes in his possession will be dealt with according to the instructions of a magistrate. Penalty for failing to comply with the requirements of this Ordinance, a fine of £25, or in default three months' imprisonment.

(NOTE. Government Notice No. 340 of 1925 gives details of the agreement between the Rhodesian Government and that of Portuguese East Africa, regarding recruitment in the Tete District of Moçambique. This is permitted to the number of 15,000 per mensem. A Portuguese Curator of Natives is established at Salisbury, who is to be paid at the rate of £1 per recruit; the Rhodesian Government guarantee that the amount shall be at least £4,500 per annum. Arrangements for payment of customs dues, and for repatriation, are included. Half-wages are to be paid on return of the labourers to Moçambique.)

The principal legislation on labour in Sierra Leone consists of the Manual Labour Regulations. Cap. 120 of the Laws (Ordinances 17 of 1905, 16 of 1908, and that of July 24, 1924). These are applied as required by Government Order (No. 21 of 1924 applied the regulations to the greater part of the colony).

The *Contract* may be by the job, or weekly for mechanics and labourers, or monthly for servants and boatmen. *Penal Sanctions*. Failure to complete contract, a fine of £2 or in default one month's imprisonment; the Courts may adjust and set off claims. Dismissal before expiry of contract entitles the employee to wages for the duration of the contract unless the Court varies this. *Crimping* is punishable with a fine of £5 or in default imprisonment for one month.

Payment is in sterling unless otherwise stipulated.

A Tribal Ruler is authorized to apply to the Courts on behalf of an aggrieved labourer, when a summons may be granted free.

Foreign Contracts. Cap. 133. (Ordinances 25 of 1931, 1 of 1914, 2 and 12 of 1924.) The provisions of the Sierra Leone Law on these will be found to be substantially the same as those of the Nigerian Code (which see). The principal differences are as follows: the approving magistrate is not required to satisfy himself that the recruit is not avoiding tribal obligations; there is a capitation fee of two shillings and sixpence per head.

Apprenticeship. Cap. 9 of the Laws (Ordinance of 1924) establishes a Board for the control of apprenticeship. Any 'minor' may, with his own consent and that of his guardian, be apprenticed, the duration not to exceed five years. The bond is cancelled if the master removes further than five miles from the place originally stipulated. Penalty for an apprentice deserting, refusing to obey orders, damaging tools, or disclosing his master's secrets, a fine of £10 and/or three months' imprisonment. A master ill-treating an apprentice is liable to a fine of £10 and/or three months' imprisonment. A master may inflict punishment amounting to six strokes on an apprentice under 16 years of age.

Forced Labour. Cap. 170 of the Laws, sections 10 to 18, authorizes the Governor to regulate the rights of chiefs and headmen to a supply of labour for purposes of public utility, or for the benefit of the native authorities. Chiefs have a right to a supply of labour for the upkeep of their farms and compounds, so long as the people are left sufficient leisure for the cultivation of their own crops. Chiefs may, with the approval of the District Commissioner, commute the right to labour for a payment in produce.

Pass Law. Cap. 170 of the Laws, Part VII, regulates the movement of natives. None may leave his chiefdom without the permission of the tribal authorities, under a penalty of a fine of £10. Chiefs may insist upon return to the chiefdom. An appeal lies to the District Commissioner, who may grant a permit to leave if refusal 'tends to interfere with trade, the labour market, or the welfare and prospects of the natives'.

SWAZILAND

The law relating to labour in Swaziland is based on Proclamation No. 19 of 1913, No. 30 of 1917, and Regulations under the High Commissioner's Notices No. 53 of 1913, No. 76 of 1917, and No. 5 of 1928.

(NOTE. Swaziland being a labour-exporting country, from which men go to work mainly in the Union of South Africa, except for some required in the local tin works, the control and welfare of workers depend on the regulations in force outside Swaziland; this accounts for the absence of rules and organization which might otherwise be expected.)

Contract. Labour agents must enter into a written contract with every recruit, to be attested before a government official; length of time is limited to 360 *working days*. All recruits must be over the apparent age of 18 *years*. *Advances* are limited to £5 exclusive of rail fares and taxes. A voluntary deferred wage system is reported to be working satisfactorily. Any contract may be cancelled by the Resident Commissioner for the following reasons: that the native is infirm; that the employer is unable to pay the wages due; that the employer has failed to provide regular employment; that the employer has brought a frivolous charge against the employee. Natives employed in the Swaziland mines are as a rule non-contract.

Forced Labour. Limited to certain tribal obligations.

Pass Law. Not in force in Swaziland.

Penal Sanctions. Penalties of a fine of £10 or two months' imprisonment are provided for any native who deserts, causes injury to property, accepts a second advance while the first is owing, or neglects to perform work which it was his duty to perform; unfits himself for work, uses abusive language to his employer, or commits any breach of rules for good order. Penalties of a fine of £50 or six months' imprisonment are also provided for persons who withhold wages; imitate the uniform of any military or police force; attempt to induce chiefs to assist in recruiting; and for native chiefs who attempt to influence prospective recruits.

Recruiting. Licensed private recruiters only. The licence is issued by the Resident Commissioner, security of £100 being required from the agent, for retention up to six months after expiration or cancellation of licence. Authorized runners only may be employed by agents, who shall carry a statement showing the proposed employer, place of employment, rate of pay, nature of work, whether food and quarters are supplied free, and period of engagement. No labour agent or runner shall engage in the sale of liquor. Recruiting is not permitted within a township, or on private property without the permission of the owner. *Penalty* for infringing regulations, a fine of £50 or six months' imprisonment.

Welfare Measures. On places of employment in Swaziland, medical or other authorized officers may enter to inspect the sanitary conditions.

Child Welfare. Recruiting is limited to persons of the age of 18 years or over.

TANGANYIKA TERRITORY

The principal labour legislation of the Tanganyika Mandated Territory is contained in the Master and Native Servants Law (Cap. 51 of the Laws, from Ordinances 32 of 1923, 11 of 1926, and 9 of 1927; Ordinance 5 of 1931 further amended Cap. 51).

Foreign Contracts must be in writing and must receive the Governor's approval; penalty for decoying natives out of the Territory without contract, fine of £100 and/or one year's imprisonment; this does not apply in the case of domestic servants.

Contracts for thirty days or less may be oral; contracts for more than thirty days must be in writing, though the making of a contract is not compulsory. Duration may be for two years, though this is restricted by Governor's proclamation to one year. Written contracts must be signed by a magistrate, certifying that he has read over and explained the conditions, and warned the servant that he is liable to criminal prosecution for breach. Wages must be paid in currency, at intervals of not more than one month. The contract must show, in addition to particulars of names, &c., the nature and duration of the work, the place of employment, and rate of pay. If he consider it necessary, an administrative officer attesting a contract may require a bond which may amount to one hundred shillings for each labourer, from the employer. *Medical inspection* was made compulsory for all contract labour by the Ordinance of 1928; fee one shilling per recruit examined, perquisite of the medical officer; penalty for failing to have men examined, fine of £100 or in default six months' imprisonment. A contract for 'thirty working days' or less may be oral. This contract expires in twice the number of working days; six days' absence constitutes desertion and breach; a 'labour card' must be given to the employee—showing names and particulars of master and servant, place, date, nature of work, rate of pay, duration of contract; this must be entered up daily, to show performance of work; the card is the property of the servant, in whose possession it must remain; it is producible evidence in court. Penalty for infringement of this section of the law, fine of £10.

Care of Servants. Housing, food, and medical attention must be provided by the employer; clothing must be provided at the request of the servant, subject to repayment by the latter.

Deaths, or injuries entailing absence from work for seven days, must be notified to the nearest administrative officer.

Repatriation expenses and food for the journey must be provided by the employer.

Compensation for injury or death may amount to two years' wages (except for cases of disobedience of specific order, or wilful misconduct). The amount is fixed by the Court, in accordance with the particulars of the case.

Safety rules relating to boilers, machinery, &c., may be made by the Governor.

Children. (Employment of children under 16 on machinery is prohibited by Government Notice No. 46 of 1927, under penalty of a fine of £50.)

Penal Sanctions. Minor Offences by Servants. Failure to begin work, or desertion; drunkenness while at work; using vehicle without permission; abusive language to employer or overseer; refusing to obey a lawful order; giving a false name or address in a contract. Penalty, a fine of half a month's wages, or in default one month's imprisonment.

Major Offences by Servants. Loss or damage of employer's property through wilful neglect or drunkenness; herdsman failing to report death or loss of animal in his charge; desertion with intent not to return; desertion while an advance of wages is owing. Penalty, fine of £5 and/or imprisonment for six months. (The Ordinance of 1928 authorized imprisonment for major offences only in default of payment of fine. It also authorized fines by employers up to half a month's wages for offences against rules for sanitation or safety, or for failure to attend hospital when instructed to do so; a record of fines to be kept, and proceeds to be forwarded to the Labour Commissioner for inclusion in a fund for the betterment of labour conditions.)

Offences by Employers. 'Withholding' wages; detaining a servant's property; failure to supply the requisites specified in the contract; non-compliance with the requirements of the law as to the care of servants. Penalty, fine of £10 and/or one month's imprisonment. (The Ordinance of 1931 substituted the words 'failure to pay' for 'withholding' wages, on the part of a master.)

Giving a reward to a headman for assistance in recruiting is punishable by a fine of £50.

Juveniles under 16 may be whipped with a cane in lieu of imprisonment, at the discretion of the Court.

Inspection of premises to ensure observance of requirements regarding care and welfare of servants was authorized by the Ordinance of 1923 in the case of administrative and medical officers; orders relating to sanitation and food might be issued, and servants might be sent to hospital at the expense of the employer.

Labour agents were required by the Ordinance of 1923 to obtain permits from District Officers, the Ordinance of 1928 transferred the issue of permits to the Labour Commissioner, and authorized the demand of a bond for £100; agents had to be persons of good character, possessing certain qualifications of education and experience, and able to produce evidence of adequate organization for care and transport of their recruits. The Ordinance of 1931 transferred the issue of permits to the Provincial Commissioners.

Labour Department. The Masters and Native Servants Ordinance of 1928 constituted a special Labour Department, which had already been formed as a result of a detailed report on labour conditions, with covering dispatch from the Governor to the

Secretary of State (Colonial No. 19 of 1926, H.M.'s Stationery Office), Labour administration was centralized under a Labour Commissioner, to whom were transferred the issue of recruiter's licences and similar duties; Labour Officers were appointed to undertake special duties, with the powers conferred by the Ordinance of 1923 on administrative and medical officers. Ordinance 35 of 1931 abolished the Labour Department, and transferred its work to the administration; Provincial Commissioners assumed the duties of the former Labour Commissioner, except for certain functions carried out by the Secretariat.

Other Legislation bearing upon Labour Questions.

Employment of Porters restriction Ordinance (No. 18 of 1928, Cap. 27 of the Laws). This authorized the Governor to proclaim by schedule any roads on which porter transport was prohibited.

Destitute Persons Ordinance (No. 1 of 1923, Cap. 32 of the Laws). Persons without visible and sufficient means of support may, under the provisions of this Ordinance, be brought before a magistrate, and ordered to find work, or detained for one month while suitable work is sought, or returned to the home district. Penalty for failure to undertake work, a fine of £5 or three months' imprisonment; for failure to return home in accordance with order, a fine of £10 or six months' imprisonment.

Native Authority Ordinance (No. 18 of 1926, Cap. 47 of the Laws). This authorizes chiefs or other authorities to call out labour (which must be paid at the ruling local rate) for essential public services, up to sixty days in the year; also, to require cultivation to ensure an adequate food-supply in case of any threat of dearth. Penalty for disobedience, fine of £10 or two months' imprisonment.

Credit to Natives Ordinance (No. 6 of 1923, Cap. 48 of the Laws). This prevents any debt from being legally recoverable from a native unless previously approved in writing by an administrative officer. (Ordinance 16 of 1931 sanctions the advance by an employer of one month's wages and the price of the servant's tax.)

Native Liquor Ordinance (No. 23 of 1923, Cap. 49 of the Laws). This requires a license for the sale of native liquor, and regulates the business; payment of wages on licensed premises to any but employees is prohibited. Penalty for breach, a fine of £20, or for second offence, a fine of £50 or three months' imprisonment.

The law relating to labour in Uganda is based mainly on Cap. 55 of the Laws (Ordinance 19 of 1913, 2 of 1919, 12 of 1920, 3 of 1923, and 19 of 1925, with further amendments in 1 of 1929).

Foreign Contract of service. Must be in writing, and must receive the Governor's consent; a fee of two shillings is chargeable; penalty for decoying away without contract, a fine of £100 or one year's imprisonment.

The Contract of Work in Uganda may be oral up to thirty working days, (introduced by Ordinance 15 of 1923). For longer periods it must be written. It must specify nature, duration, and place of work, wages (which must be paid at intervals of not more than one month) and the usual particulars of employer and servant. Limit, two years. The Masters and Native Servants Amendment Ordinance, No. 1 of 1929, introduces a year's written contract, for a number of working days not less than five-sevenths of the total duration of the contract. In the case of such contracts it is further stipulated that the employer must provide food.

Apprenticeship is authorized for youths between the ages of 9 and 16 ,with the approval of the guardian, or in the case of destitutes a magistrate. Agreements must be in writing, and must be approved by a magistrate.

Crimping is punishable with a fine of £20 or two months' imprisonment.

Welfare. Labourers must be 'properly' housed; medical attention must be provided; hospital fees 'during illness' must be paid.

Illness or death must be notified to the local administrative officer.

Repatriation must be provided under conditions similar to those of recruitment, and food for the journey must be given.

Recruiting. Labour agents must have a permit from the Provincial Commissioner (Government Notice of November 11, 1919, substituted District, for Provincial, Commissioner). A bond may be required for an amount to be fixed by the Provincial Commissioner. Permits are valid for twelve months. Assistants must be registered, and a list of employers served must be produced. All recruits must be placed on contract. The definition of a labour agent excludes the private employer recruiting for his own business. Penalty for infringement of recruiting regulations, fine of £100 or one year's imprisonment.

Disputes may be heard by first or second-class courts, which can vary the terms of contracts where this is desirable. Civil procedure may be followed at discretion.

Penal Sanctions. Minor Offences by Servants. Failure to begin work after contracting; absence from work; drunkenness; carelessness; using a vehicle without permission; abusive language to employer or headman; refusal to obey a lawful order; giving a false name or address on contracting. Punishment, a fine of one month's wages, or one month's imprisonment.

Major Offences. Loss of property of employer through wilful breach of duty or drunkenness; jeopardizing safety of property by the same means; herdsman failing to report death or loss of animal in his charge; fraudulent alleged loss of property; desertion with intent not to return. Offences are cognizable, and police may arrest without warrant. Penalty, a fine of £7 10s. 0d. or six months' imprisonment. Compensation for loss occasioned by servant may be awarded to the employer by the Court.

Desertion while an advance of wages is owing is punishable with a fine of £25 or three months' imprisonment.

Offences by employers. 'Withholding' wages; detaining the property of a servant; failing to supply food or other articles as stipulated in the contract; failing to comply with the legal requirements as to health and welfare; punishment, a fine of £10 or one month's imprisonment. The fine is payable to the complainant at the discretion of the Court.

Inspection. Any magistrate may inspect premises where labourers work or live, to ensure that the requirements of the law are being carried out.

Regulations for the better observance of the terms of the law may be made by the Governor.

Other Legislation bearing upon Labour Matters.

Forced Labour. The Native Authority Law, Cap. 60 (Ordinances 17 of 1919, 8 of 1921, and 33 of 1931) empowers chiefs to require work from able-bodied adult males, for the benefit of the community; the duration must not exceed thirty days in the year. Compulsion may also be resorted to for porterage or labour for public works; this must not exceed sixty days, while three months' previous employment in the year exempts; payment at the local ruling rate must be made. District Commissioners, with the

Governor's sanction, may issue orders to chiefs relating to compulsory cultivation or relief work in case of famine. The provisions of the Masters and Servants Ordinances apply to this labour. The Governor may commute this obligation in any manner that may seem to him desirable. Penalty for refusal to comply with such orders, a fine of £7 10s. 0d. or two months' imprisonment.

Poll Tax. Cap. 53 of the Laws (Ordinances 27 of 1920, 22 of 1921, 6 of 1922, and 3 of 1923). Failure to pay this tax renders the defaulter liable to work for government up to two months.

Native Liquor. Cap. 111 of the Laws (Ordinance 9 of 1916). The sale of native liquor is regulated and must be licensed; the Governor may make rules for further regulation.

The Finger-Print Law. Cap. 33 of the Laws (Ordinance 28 of 1922). This applies only to criminals.

Porterage. Cap. 55 of the Laws (Ordinance 1 of 1913) regulates conditions of porterage, and restricts the load to 60 lb.

(NOTE. This law provides no powers of restricting the use of porterage.)

The Factories Law. Cap. 109 of the Laws (Ordinance 23 of 1919; Rule No. 3 of 1928 also applies). This establishes a Board for the regulation of conditions in factories and workshops; the said Board consists of the Director of Public Works, the Director of Agriculture, the Chief Sanitation Officer, and such other members as may be deemed necessary. The Governor is authorized to make rules for the safety and health of workers, the prevention of accidents, the regulation of hours and nature of buildings, and for the appointing of factory inspectors. Inspecting officers may order the remedying of defective or dangerous buildings or equipment. Penalty for infringement, a fine of £100 or twelve months' imprisonment.

Employment of Children. (Ordinance No. 13 of 1930). This refers to factories and workshops. Employment of children under 12 years of age is forbidden; children between the ages of 12 and 14 may be employed with the authorization of the Factories Board. A table of the hours of work must be sent to the Board, and these may not exceed eight hours daily with one hour's rest. The Board's licence to employ children must be posted in the factory. Inspection by medical and administrative officers and by factory inspectors is authorized to ensure observance of the law. Accidents are notifiable to the Board and to a police officer. The Governor is authorized to make further rules for regulating the use of child labour. Penalty for infringement, a fine of £50 or twelve months' imprisonment.

Employment of Women. (Ordinance 32 of 1931.) This is prohibited at night, except in emergency due to the nature of the material or work. Inspection is authorized by medical and administrative officers and factory inspectors. The Governor may make rules for the better protection of women workers. Penalty for breach of this law, a fine of £20 or six months' imprisonment.

Vagrancy. (Ordinances 2 of 1909, 19 of 1922, and 19 of 1930.) A vagrant is any person found wandering without employment or visible means of support. Police may arrest without warrant, when the case is triable in a second-class court, and a magistrate may commit an offender to jail up to three months. Vagrants are to receive the same prison treatment as others of their nationality, but are not to wear prison dress or be lodged with criminals. The Commissioner of Prisons is to provide work for which wages are to be paid, to form a fund for the return of the vagrant to his home.

Penalty for non-compliance with a magistrate's order, or escape from custody, three months' imprisonment, or for a subsequent offence six months.

Under Ordinance 19 of 1930 vagrants under the age of 16 may be returned to their guardians; if again found wandering, they may be punished with six strokes with the cane.

UNION OF SOUTH AFRICA

Labour laws made an early appearance in the legislation of South Africa, and the following summary will give a general idea of the long development that has taken place.

In 1828 Ordinance 49 regulated the manner of employment of free labourers, and provided for the furnishing of passes. Order in Council of August 27, 1842, regulated the relations of Masters, Servants, and Apprentices. The Cape Act No. 27 of 1857 introduced a five-year contract. Transvaal Law No. 9 of 1870 restricted squatters to five families, and Law No. 4 of 1873 required every native to procure an annual pass, cost £1, remitted on burgher's certificate of six months' employment. In 1895 'Labour Districts' were constituted, a two-shilling monthly pass being established; record of contracts was provided for, and inspectors were appointed to supervise and hear complaints from masters and servants.

Recruiting in 'Labour Districts' was prohibited. In 1907 the Transvaal established the Government Native Labour Bureau, in view of the repatriation of Chinese indentured labour.

The principal provincial legislation concerning labour consists of (a) *The Cape Province* Masters and Servants Acts, 1856 to 1889; these apply to most manual labour, including agriculture and domestic service; they sanction oral contracts up to one year, and written contracts up to five years; provisions for contract of wife or child are included. (b) *Natal*. The Masters and Servants Act No. 40 of 1894 provides for attestation of contract before an official, and limits the contract to three years. (c) *The Transvaal*. Law No. 13 of 1880. The definition of 'servant' was widened by Act 27 of 1909, and Act 26 of 1926, to cover land tenants. The provisions governing contracts are similar to those of the Cape. (d) *The Orange Free State*. Ordinance No. 7 of 1904; oral contracts limited to one year, written contracts to two years, if attested before a magistrate. Provision for the service of wife or child as in the Cape.

Provincial legislation still holds good, but the following laws of the Union regulate the existing labour situation:

Act 15 of 1911, Native Labour Regulations, authorized the issue of regulations by the Governor-General regarding accommodation, medical attention, and diet scales, with especial reference to the mines, agriculture not being included.

Wages Protection Act, 15 of 1914, makes wages due a first charge on money payable to a contractor, and protects wages against assignment or attachment.

Workmen's Compensation Act, 25 of 1914, established compensation for injuries or occupational diseases incurred during employment.

The Factory Act, 28 of 1918, limits working hours, overtime, and employment of women and juveniles.

The Juveniles Act, 33 of 1921, established supervision and guidance for scholars leaving school; virtually non-native in scope.

The Industrial Conciliation Act, 11 of 1924, establishes conciliation machinery, but its provisions make it largely inapplicable to native labour, nor does it apply to agriculture or domestic service.

The Wages Act, 27 of 1925 (amended by Acts 21 and 23 of 1930) supplements the foregoing, and establishes conciliation machinery with representatives of employers and employees; it does not apply to agriculture or domestic service, and deals largely with Trade Unions.

The Miners' Phthisis Acts consolidated by Act 35 of 1925, provides compensation for native patients, but on a different footing from that for non-natives.

The Department of Labour was enlarged in 1924 to deal with (1) employment generally, including government works and unemployment relief; (2) training of the poor and unemployed; (3) conciliation boards and registry offices, &c.; (4) wages acts; (5) juvenile affairs; (6) apprenticeship; (7) factories; (8) workmen's compensation; (9) social welfare; (10) International Labour Office Affairs.

Labour Exchanges for facilitating employment were set up in the larger towns, their activities utilizing also the Post Office organization.

The Native Labour Regulation Act of 1911 conferred powers on the Director of Native Labour to deal with the following matters: (1) Control of recruiting and issue of licences; (2) issue of licences to compound managers; (3) right of prosecution of licence holders; (4) supervision of payment of native wages; (5) assessment of payment of compensation for native labourers; (6) power to cancel contracts; (7) control of repatriation; (8) right to inspect employers' records of wages paid; (9) right to require employers and labour agents to furnish returns of labourers; (10) control of housing, feeding, medical attention, and hospital accommodation for labourers.

Trade unions generally maintain a definite colour bar, and the Industrial and Commercial Workers' Union, established in 1919, for natives, is not affiliated to others, Indian workers having separate organizations. (NOTE. In 1929, Indians were admitted to membership of the Typographical Union.) In July, 1924, the Prime Minister issued a Circular to all departments with instructions to the effect that, wherever possible, civilized labour should be utilized in the government services in place of that which may be classed as uncivilized. 'Civilized labour' is defined as labour rendered by persons whose standard of living generally conforms to and is recognized as tolerable from a European standpoint.

Recapitulation according to subject.

Workmen's Compensation. Act 15 of 1911, Native Labour Regulations section 22, refers to accidents; Act 25 of 1914 provides compensation for injury incurred during employment. The Miners' Phthisis Act, 35 of 1925, amended by Act 38 of 1930, provides compensation for native workers who contract that disease.

Contracts. (See also, Recruiting, *infra*.) Cape Province: oral, up to one year; written, up to five years. Natal: contracts limited to three years. Transvaal; similar to the Cape. Orange Free State: oral, up to one year; written, up to two years. Contracts are permissive, as is attestation before a magistrate, but the Native Labour Regulation Act, 15 of 1911, section 12, requires labour agents to enter into a contract with every native recruited by them, and enforces attestation before a magistrate. 'Attestation' takes place on engagement, 'registration of contract' takes place on the native beginning work, and is effected by a registering officer authorized by the Director of Labour, the employer being liable to fine for omission. Contracts are in triplicate, one for the attesting officer, one for the agent, and one for the conductor of the labourers for surrender to the registering officer. Section 12 of the Native Labour Regulation Act prohibits attestation in the case of any native apparently under the age of 18.

Advances. The Native Advances Act, 18 of 1921 (regulations issued by Proclamation 175 of 1921, and 231 of 1923), restricts advances to £2, or £3 in case of contracts for more than nine months.

Payment in Cash. The Native Labour Regulation Act, 15 of 1911, in a definition, refers to 'cash or any substitute therefor' and Union legislation generally does not clearly require payment of wages in cash.

Medical Examination. The Director of Labour may prohibit the employment of any person medically unfit; special regulations in the Transvaal, the Orange Free State, and the Labour districts of Natal, require vaccination and medical examination before the labourer begins work (Regulations 26 and 30 of 1911).

Forced Labour. Not legal in the Union of South Africa. In Natal the Locust Extermination Act of 1904 introduces a small element of compulsion in connexion with anti-locust measures.

Pass Laws. These are in force in all provinces except the Cape; diversity of the provisions renders consolidating legislation difficult.

Penal Sanctions. Contravention of the Native Labour Regulations Act entails a fine up to £50 or in default imprisonment up to six months where no penalty is specified; where the penalty is specified, the fine is up to £10, or in default, up to three months' imprisonment. Offences are: by the employer, withholding wages. By the employee; desertion, injury to property, or accepting an advance from more than one agent. Inspectors may fine employees up to £2 for neglecting to perform work, drunkenness, refusal to obey a lawful command, abusive language to employer, or infringing safety regulations.

Recruiting. Carried on by officially recognized organizations, labour agents, and employers. Licences consist of (*a*) a labour agent's licence, (*b*) an employer's recruiting licence, (*c*) a conductor's licence, and (*d*) a runner's permit. The labour agent's costs £5 to £50 according to scope; the employer's and conductor's cost £1 each. Labour agents must deposit a guarantee of £200, retained until six months after the expiration of the licence. Clothing, feeding, and transport are arranged by the recruiting organizations, the Director of Native Labour having control of licences, and being empowered to supervise arrangements. Section 13 of the Native Labour Regulation Act, 15 of 1911, prohibits recruiting by threat, or by resort to the help of headmen; penalizes misrepresentation of the nature of the employment; penalizes crimping; prohibits recruiting on private land without the owner's permission, or on railway premises without the sanction of the Director of Labour; penalizes the offering of liquor to secure recruits.

Women and Children. Contracts may not be made with persons under the age of 18. The Factories Act, 28 of 1918, prohibits factory employment of children under 12, and regulates conditions for those under 16, and for women, prohibiting night work for these. Maternity protection prohibits employment four weeks before, or eight weeks after childbirth. Act 29 of 1918 regulates wages of women and young persons in industry.

ZANZIBAR

Earlier legislation on the subject of labour was repealed by the Masters and Servants Decree, of December 14, 1925, which was a measure largely in accordance with the practice in other East African territories. The principal provisions are as follows.

Foreign Contracts. These must be approved by the Resident, who may exact a bond for Rs.200 for performance of obligations. Return passage for labourers is secured.

Contracts. In Zanzibar these may be oral for one month, but must be written for a longer period; they must be concluded before a magistrate, who is to explain the conditions to the labourer. Limit, two years. They must specify the nature and duration of the employment, the place and the rate of wage, and an undertaking to pay wages at intervals of not less than one month. Certain details refer to the peculiarities of the clove-picking industry.

Crimping is punishable with a fine of Rs.1,000 or six months' imprisonment.

Housing is subject to the sanitary requirements of administrative and medical officers. Deaths must be at once notified to the nearest administrative officer.

Costs of return journey to place of recruitment are secured.

The ordinary *Courts* have jurisdiction to deal with labour cases; they may order the arrest of any absconding defendant, and may regulate or adjust the terms of contracts according to the nature of complaints received. Either criminal or civil procedure may be followed.

Offences by servants are: failure to begin work after contract; absence; drunkenness; carelessness; use of any vehicle without permission; abusive language to employer or headman; refusal to obey a lawful order; giving a false name or address on engagement. These are punishable with a fine of half a month's wages, or in default one month's imprisonment. The employer may be compensated from a servant's wages for loss caused through his fault. Desertion while an advance is owing is punishable with a fine of Rs.100 or six months' imprisonment.

Offences by employers consist of withholding wages, detaining the property of a servant, and failing to carry out the legal requirements for the welfare of the servant. The Resident is authorized to make rules for the betterment of labour conditions.

The Apprenticeship Decree No. 15 of 1926, authorized the apprenticeship of any Arab or African young person between the ages of 9 and 16, by his guardian, with his consent. A District Commissioner may act in place of a guardian in the case of a destitute child; the transaction must be carried out before a District Commissioner. No apprentice may be removed from Zanzibar, under penalty of a fine of Rs. 500 or six months' imprisonment. Crimping of apprentices is punishable with a fine of Rs.250 or three months' imprisonment. The provisions of the Masters and Servants Decree apply to apprentices.

The Native Seamen's Decree. No. 37 of 1925, requires all engagements of seamen to take place before the Port Officer, except for coastal journeys; a bond for the proper observance of the conditions of the agreement may be required. Penalty for infringement of this Decree, a fine of Rs.1,000 or six months' imprisonment.

Other Legislation referring to Labour.

Slavery. The Slave Trade was prohibited on August 1, 1890, and slavery abolished, July 7, 1897.

Forced Labour. The Employment of Natives Decree, December 4, 1923, amended December 12, 1923, authorized a District Officer to call upon any able-bodied adult male native to work on services of public utility; this is limited to sixty days in the year, and occupation in other employment exempts. For porterage, the District Officer may exercise his own authority; for employment on roads, bridges, railways, government buildings, harbours, telegraphs, and other works, the previous sanction of the Secretary of State must be obtained for the compulsion, the period of employment being limited and specified. Decree No. 1 of 1931 repealed this Decree.

The Destitute Persons Decree, No. 12 of 1930, defines destitute persons as being those without visible and sufficient means of support. Police may arrest these without warrant, and bring them before a magistrate. The latter may (1) order them to find work; (2) detain them up to one month; (3) send them to their homes, or if they are not natives of Zanzibar, order them to be deported. Non-compliance is punishable with a fine of Rs.50, or three months' imprisonment. In case of detention under this Decree the destitute is, if confined in any prison, to be treated as a person awaiting trial. The Superintendent of the prison is to seek suitable work for the destitute, who is liable to six months' imprisonment if he should refuse to accept this when found. Juveniles may be handed over to their guardians, and may be punished with six strokes of a light cane.

The Reformation Decree of December 4, 1926, refers to youthful offenders under the age of 16; it establishes reformatories for those between the ages of 12 and 16. Police may arrest youthful vagrants without warrant, but must bring them before a magistrate within twenty-four hours. The latter may consign them to a reformatory.

The Governor of Prisons may transfer a youthful offender from a reformatory to the service of a suitable employer.

(NOTE. The *Registration of Adult Males Decree* of December 24, 1917, which required all adult native males between the ages of 15 and 65 to be registered and furnished with a certificate, was repealed by Decree No. 11 of 1928.)

NOTE. The following are the equivalents used for certain French terms: Order—Arrêté; Decree—Decret; A.G.G.—Arrêté du Gouverneur Général.

In Mandated Territories the Commissary of the Republic holds an office equivalent to that of Governor General in a Colony.

THE administration of the French Colonies being to a large extent centralized, regulations regarding labour are generally common to all, appropriate Decrees applying the law to each individual country, with such local modifications as may be necessary. The following is a summary of the existing position.

Forced Labour. Abolished. There is, however, still the 'native contingent' (*contingent indigène*) in Madagascar and West Africa, which is a species of military service, justified on the same grounds as is general conscription. There is also the 'régime des prestations' which is a form of tax payable in labour. This is limited to fifteen days a year, which must not fall in the seasons for planting and harvesting; it is limited to works of public utility near the homes of the workers; a daily food ration is provided, and special exemptions exclude certain classes on account of age, sex, military or official occupation, &c. Substitution of a cash payment in lieu of work is permitted.

Principal legislation on the subject of labour is, for West Africa, the Decree of April 24, 1928; for Madagascar, the Decree of September 22, 1925; for the Cameroons, the Decree of August 4, 1922, completed by the Decrees of July 9, 1925 and February 15, 1926; recruiting is regulated by a local proclamation of February 18, 1921. For Togoland, the Decree of December 29, 1922, completed by the orders of the Commissary of the Republic dated May 25, 1923, October 27, 1924, and December 12, 1925. Emigration was regulated by the Decree of March 1, 1927.

Main Provisions of the Law.

Emigration. Recruitment and transport of workers outside the colony is prohibited without the authorization of the Governor.

Immigration. In Madagascar this is regulated and encouraged by an immigration service, established by the Decree of May 6, 1903.

Recruiting. In West Africa the recruitment of workers intended for employment in the colony does not require any administrative sanction. In Equatorial Africa recruiters must be authorized by the local administration; recruiting may only be carried on in areas where it is permitted, and it is limited to a certain proportion of adult males, these two restrictions being adjusted annually by the Governor (Decree of May 4, 1922, and A.G.G. of February 11, 1923. In Madagascar recruiting requires no authorization, but it can be suspended by an Order of the Governor General, for reasons of public welfare, health, &c. (Decree of September 22, 1925.)

Labour Offices. In West Africa, the A.G.G. of March 29, 1926, and in Madagascar, the Decree of September 22, 1925, established Labour Offices. These form official bureaux for employment, information, and statistics; they serve as intermediaries between employers and workers, facilitate recruiting, and control labour . contracts.

Medical Examination. Compulsory and free in every French African colony, before any contract is signed.

Transport. In all colonies, the cost of transport and repatriation between the place of engagement and that of employment, are a charge on the employer. Regulations for food, accommodation, medical attention, &c., *en route*, are made by the Governor.

Contract. Entire freedom in contracting is assured. Engagements for a period exceeding three months in West and Equatorial Africa or one month in Madagascar, must be the subject of a contract. Duration is limited to two years. (West Africa, Decree of October 22, 1925; Equatorial Africa, Decree of May 4, 1922; Madagascar, Decree of September 22, 1925.

Details of Contract. Full name, nationality, profession, and residence of the employer; full name, age, and sex of the employee, and the names of his village, chief, and district, also any identification marks; the exact nature of the work, and the place where it is to be performed; duration of contract; wages, with the periods and mode of payment, including, in the case of piecework, a minimum wage; detailed scale of food ration; provision for clothing and housing; medical certificate of fitness; a declaration by the employee that he is free from other obligations; an undertaking by the employer to facilitate payment of taxes by his employee; and any special provisions. (West Africa, Decree of October 22, 1925; Madagascar, Decree of September 22, 1923; Equatorial Africa, Decree of May 4, 1922, which also requires that contracts should comply with a prescribed form.)

Formalities to be observed. Contracts must be in French; three copies are made, one for the employer, the second for the servant, and the third for the administrative office. (West Africa, Decree of October 22, 1925; Madagascar, Decree of September 22, 1925; in Equatorial Africa, contracts are carried out by the administrative authorities.)

Identity Book. This must be given to the employee on engagement; it must comply with a prescribed form, and must contain a copy of any contract. (*Livret d'identité*, West Africa, A.G.G. of March 29, 1926; *livre de travail*, Equatorial Africa, Decree of May 4, 1922, A.G.G. of February 11, 1923; A.G.G. of January 3, 1927; Madagascar, Decree of September 22, 1925.)

Cancellation of Contract and Desertion. Desertion is no longer regarded as a crime; the regulations distinguish between legitimate and illegitimate absence. It is legitimate when it results from permit, sickness, visit to any official, or other good reason; it entails the loss of wages, but the employee is entitled to food and lodging. Absence is illegitimate when it is merely the result of the employee's inclination; in this case it entails breach of the contract and liability in civil law. (West Africa, Decree of October 22, 1925, and A.G.G. of March 29, 1926. Equatorial Africa, Decree of April 7, 1911, A.G.G. of February 11, 1923. Madagascar, Decree of September 22, 1925.)

Penal Sanctions. The law makes the following acts criminal: (*a*) the completion of a fictitious contract; (*b*) dissuasion of any prospective employee from contracting, by the use of threats or promises; (*c*) persuading any employee to break his contract, by the same means; (*d*) knowingly pleading a contract which is not applicable; (*e*) accepting other employment when under contract. The infractions are punishable with imprisonment and fine; in West Africa there may be in addition, for the offending employer, a suspension of his right to engage labourers. (West Africa, Decree of October 22, 1925; Equatorial Africa, Decree of May 4, 1922; Madagascar, Decree of September 22, 1925.)

Vagabondage. In Madagascar, the Decree of August 28, 1921, renders native vagabonds liable to three months, up to a year, in prison; they are defined as natives who have no regular means of support, or who are without definite domicile.

Arbitration Councils. (Conseils d'arbitrage.) The Law has transferred the consideration of disputes over labour contracts from the ordinary courts to special bodies. These Arbitration

Councils deal with all differences arising out of conditions of employment. As a rule, the local administrative officer is the President; he is assisted by assessors who consist of colonists and natives in equal numbers. (West Africa, Decree of October 22, 1925; Equatorial Africa, Decree of May 4, 1922; Madagascar, Decree of September 22, 1925.)

Child Labour. An age-limit for employment is fixed by the administrative authority in each colony; it varies between 15 and 20 years, according to the nature of the work.

Female Labour. In West Africa, A.G.G. of March 29, 1926, entitles native women workers to eight weeks' maternity leave, during which they are entitled to a food ration and half wages. In Madagascar, Decree of September 22, 1925 prohibited the employment of women between nine o'clock at night and five o'clock in the morning.

Hours of Work. Generally, the working-day consists of ten hours which must include the time spent between the place of employment and the living quarters; this rule applies to employees in agriculture as well as to those in industry. In Equatorial Africa the hours of work for employees on first engagement must not exceed six per diem for the first month, and eight per diem for the second month, of the engagement. (West Africa, A.G.G. of March 29, 1926; Equatorial Africa, A.G.G. February 11, 1923; Madagascar, Decree of September 22, 1925.)

Rest Periods. Two hours' rest must be permitted at midday; a weekly day of rest must be allowed, and public holidays must be observed. (Authorities, as for the previous section.)

Minimum Rate of Wage. The rate of pay must not be below a minimum fixed by an Order of the Governor for each colony; payment must be in cash, and not in kind or in goods; it must be made at stated periods, at least once a month. (Authorities as for the previous section.)

Advances. The only advances authorized are those agreed upon at the time of engagement, when the attesting official can determine the sum and the periods of repayment; special penalties are attached to the fraudulent obtaining of advances. (West Africa, A.G.G. of October 22, 1925 and Decree of June 6, 1911, referring to fraudulent advances. Equatorial Africa, Decree of April 14, 1920. Madagascar, Decree of September 22, 1925, and for fraudulent advances, Decree of November 7, 1911.

Deductions and Savings. Deductions from salaries can only be made in accordance with regulations, for return of an advance, payment of tax, or in accordance with a decision of an Arbitration Council. (West Africa, A.G.G. of March 29, 1926; Equatorial Africa, A.G.G. of February 11, 1923; Madagascar, Decree of September 22, 1925.)

Arrangements exist for helping the labourer to accumulate savings payable at the end of his contract, at his home; payments are made in the form of monthly deductions, with which are purchased 'saving stamps' (*timbres pécules*) which are put in a 'savings book' (*carnet de pécule*) opened in the name of each worker. (West Africa, Decree of October 22, 1925; Equatorial Africa, A.G.G. of November 11, 1923.)

Food, Lodging, and Clothing of Workers. When the contract involves the employment of labourers away from their homes, they and their families must be accommodated at the expense of the employer; a certain standard is prescribed by law, relating to matters of hygiene, provision of drinking water, disposal of refuse, &c. Regulations also require minimum dimensions of rooms, raising of beds above the floor, &c. The employer can be called upon to carry out any improvements indicated by an Inspector of Labour. In West Africa and Madagascar, employees must be provided, at the employer's expense, with an outfit sufficient to protect them against the weather, according to a scale promulgated by administrative authority, on medical advice. In both West and Equatorial Africa, all employees have a right to a daily ration for themselves and their families. This must be in kind, on a scale detailed by the local administrative authorities. (West Africa, A.G.G. of March 29, 1926; Equatorial Africa, A.G.G. of February 11, 1923; Madagascar, Decree of September 22, 1925.)

Health. Regulations detail the organization of the medical and dispensing staff to be provided for places of employment, with the necessary hospitals and dispensaries, and the drugs that must be kept; these vary according to the number of the employees, and the standard of the particular colony. In the African colonies the doctors of the Native Medical Service make inspections to ensure the requisite standard of sanitation, accommodation, food, cleanliness, &c.; in cases where this is not satisfactory, they can order the necessary improvements to be carried out at the expense of the employer. In case of sickness or accident, the worker is entitled, for a period which varies according to the colony, to medical treatment, food, accommodation, and a part of his wages. At the end of the fixed period, the contract may be terminated, but only by reference to the Arbitration Council. In West Africa the death of the worker from any cause entitles his family to compensation at a rate determined by the administration, but at a reduced rate when death is due to a cause other than an accident or occupational disease. (West Africa, A.G.G., March 29, 1926. Equatorial Africa, A.G.G., February 11, 1923. Madagascar, Decree of September 22, 1925.)

Accidents and Occupational Diseases. In West Africa, Article 40 of A.G.G. of March 29, 1926, orders that in case of any illness or injury directly resulting from the nature of employment, the workers must receive adequate care until they recover, or are pronounced incurable, and this without prejudice to any claim under civil law. If death ensues, the family has a right to compensation. In Equatorial Africa the employer is responsible for accidents sustained by employees during working hours, at the place of employment. (Article 15 of A.G.G. of February 11, 1925.) If incapacity for work results, the employer is liable to payment of compensation fixed by the administration. In Madagascar principles of common law are applied, and the employer is responsible for injuries resulting from neglect on his part: it has been found, however, that the application of the metropolitan law of April 9, 1898, is only partially possible (*une application fragmentaire*) owing to the lack of medical services, inspectorates, &c., necessary to enforce its provisions fully, and also to the absence of Insurance Societies.

Penalties for infringement of conditions of employment. These vary according to the colony, but include fines of one to one hundred francs, with imprisonment from one day to two months.

Inspection. In Equatorial Africa the organization of the Labour Inspectorate is still rudimentary; it is carried out by administrative and medical officers who are instructed to supervise the due performance of contracts and the observance of regulations. In West Africa, and still more in Madagascar, inspection is organized with precision. The personnel of the Labour Inspectorate is carefully selected from those whose rank and experience of the country render them well qualified for the work; they receive a special appointment. They carry out tours of inspection, during which they visit all factories, workshops, and plantations employing any natives, while they also inspect camps and living accommodation; they examine all contracts and identity books, and receive any complaints or claims by employers or employees; in case of dispute, they endeavour to effect an agreement, failing which they refer the question to the Arbitration Council. They take the necessary legal action in case of infringement of regulations; and each submits an annual report on the local working of the labour laws, with any suggestions for improvements in these. (West Africa, A.G.G. March 29, 1926; Equatorial Africa, Decree of May 4, 1922, and A.G.G. of February 11, 1923; Madagascar, Decree of September 22, 1925.)

Apprenticeship. In West Africa, A.G.G. of May 1, 1924, created at Dakar an apprenticeship school. In Equatorial Africa, A.G.G. of September 13, 1926, regulated apprenticeship. In Madagascar, A.G.G. of December 20, 1910, organized industrial apprenticeship of natives, while A.G.G. of February 5, 1921, introduced professional teaching and regulated the industrial school at Tananarive. (Modifications were introduced by A.G.G. of February 27, 1924, and A.G.G. of April 23, 1926.)

(NOTE. It will be observed that in many instances French Colonial Law contains provisions largely according with the requirements of the International Draft Conventions, although these may not have been ratified by France; for instance, employment of women at night, workmen's compensation, minimum wage fixing machinery, &c.)

ITALIAN SOMALILAND AND ERITREA

THE principal legislation relating to labour in Eritrea is the Governor's Decree No. 9631 of September 1, 1916, and for Somaliland, Decree No. 8220 of July 31, 1930. These introduce some regulation of labour, though the small degree of development in the colonies renders detailed measures scarcely necessary.

District Commissioners are charged with the publication of the requirements of employers, but are prohibited from using any sort of pressure; they are entitled to refuse to allow labourers to leave their homes for work, should this seem desirable.

(NOTE. Labourers from the Sudan arrive in numbers usually adequate for all local requirements.)

Recruitment. Labour must be recruited from volunteers only. In Somaliland, Decree No. 8220 of July 31, 1930, established a Labour Bureau for each Commissioner's District ('presso ogni sede di commissariato istituito un ufficio del lavoro'). This decree requires all employers to engage their workmen through the Bureau, and to furnish a list of these in their employment.

A Labour Card (*tessera di lavoratore*) must be given to each employee, being furnished free by the administrative office, where a record of each card is to be kept.

Welfare of Labourers. Sanitation and health measures are regulated by the various rules in force in each area; special provisions are not considered necessary.

Contracts are governed by Italian law generally; a difference is made between casual labour, and contract labour, which latter must be for at least three months. Details required: the employer must furnish a return showing the personnel in his employment; dates of payment (which must be weekly); fines inflicted; and medical assistance available. Penalty for non-compliance; one month's imprisonment or a fine of 300 liras. Contracts must be concluded before an official, who must inform the employee of the details of the contract; it only becomes binding on both parties after seven days' trial work with wages.

Wages are usually to be paid in money; in certain circumstances they may, at the expressed wish of the employee, be paid in kind. In Somaliland Decree No. 8220 of July 31, 1930, introduces a classification of all labourers, and lays down a table of wage rates to be paid, ranging from 24 to 3 liras monthly, according to capacity; this scale is reviewed periodically by the Governor on the recommendation of the District Commissioners.

Penal Sanctions. Breach of contract generally is dealt with by the courts under Italian law, or local law where applicable. Imprisonment or flogging up to fifty lashes may be inflicted for grave offences. (In Eritrea Decree No. 5142 of December 19, 1930, regulates the infliction of lashes, and exempts certain classes from it.)

Fines inflicted by the employer must be entered in the work-book or card, and these are open to inspection by the District Commissioner. The proceeds of all such fines are to be forwarded to the local administrative office, for inclusion in a fund for the improvement of labour conditions.

Disputes are regulated by a specially appointed arbitrator for each district head-quarters.

LIBERIA

SERIOUS allegations of resort to forced labour, not only for Government purposes, but also for private employment, having been made, the Liberian Government appealed to the League of Nations for assistance and advice in a general reformation of methods of administration, finance, and sanitation. Subsequent investigation revealed the need for drastic changes.

It is thus impossible to give particulars of the laws and practice as regards labour in this Republic, until reorganization has been carried out.

THE regulation of labour conditions in the Portuguese Colonies has been so largely a matter for the home government that it may well be dealt with as a whole, special reference being made, where necessary, to individual colonies.

Portuguese legislation to regulate the status of slaves and mitigate their condition, makes its appearance in the eighteenth century, and a long series of laws culminated in that of April 29, 1858, enacting the freeing of all slaves within twenty years from that date. Subsequent legislation has been directed towards the regulation of free or forced labour.

The Decree of November 9, 1899, while maintaining the native's obligation to work, established supervision for recruiting, repatriation, journey conditions, medical aid, details of contracts, and similar matters, and created a special magistrature to deal with such subjects.

The Decree of May 27, 1911, limited the duration of *contracts* to two years, made corporal punishment of workers punishable by law, introduced finger-prints for contract agreements, and penalized the withholding by employers of food or wages.

The Decree of October 14, 1914, withdrew the obligation on officials to assist in recruiting, and further regulated the conditions of transport, treatment, food, and lodging of recruits. It also drew attention to the danger of *over-recruiting*, and provided for the prohibition of this where necessary. The administration is, however, instructed to encourage recruiting by all legitimate means for agricultural or commercial enterprises; officials are also entitled to recruit directly all natives who show themselves refractory to the moral and legal obligation to work. Any native who is physically fit to work, and who has not adequate visible means of support, may be recruited compulsorily by the authorities and ordered to work for three months to one year for government or for a private employer. From this regulation are exempt state employees, wage-earners, professional or commercial workers, men over sixty or under fourteen, chiefs and headmen, and women. Officials are also permitted to resort to compulsion for labour for public purposes.

Recruiting by chiefs is to be encouraged in connexion with natives who are refractory towards the obligation to work; payment *per capita* may be made to them. (This usage required implementing in the various colonies; e.g. in Portuguese Guinea, Article 104 of Arrêté No. 83 B of November 29, 1922, sanctions payment of one escudo per recruit, to native authorities.)

Professional recruiters must be licensed by the Governor of the colony; they must be persons of proved good character, and must deposit a bond for good behaviour; licences are issued for one year, are personal, and may be withdrawn at any time by the Governor, who can also limit the area of their applicability. The recruiter may employ a limited number of European and native assistants, who must be officially approved; they must also be Portuguese subjects.

The operation of *recruiting companies* is authorized, and their employees are exempted from the deposit of a bond.

Private employers requiring more than ten labourers are authorized to recruit on licence, but only in the neighbourhood of their place of business.

Domestic employment is free from regulation as to recruiting.

Transport of workers is the duty of the recruiter; professionals must take their recruits to the nearest representative of the Protector of Natives. Camps along the routes followed must be provided where food and shelter is available. It is prohibited to send natives to any locality other than that in which they have agreed to serve. Article 105 provides that the cost of transport of refractory natives who are under compulsion to work for a private employer, shall be chargeable to the employer.

Contracts. Not compulsory within the colony, except for professional recruiters; recruits, however, must be taken before an official who shall satisfy himself that they have engaged voluntarily, and that they know the conditions of employment and rate of wages. Contracts not made before an official must be communicated to the authorities. Children under 14 may not be recruited; those aged between 14 and 18 require the sanction of their parent or guardian. Contracts must be in triplicate, and one copy must be sent to the Protector of Natives. Each colony may require government approval for all contracts, and this is virtually necessitated by the fact that legal enforcement of contract is impossible without previous official approval of the terms.

Contracts are individual, as each recruit, after engagement, is given an identity card, on which the principal points of the contract are stated; should he be accompanied by his family, their names are included on this card.

The contract is signed by the employer or the recruiter, and thumb-marked by the employee, if illiterate. It is registered by the approving authority, and a copy is sent to the district office of the place of employment.

Desertion or contract breaking by a labourer who owes money for an advance is punishable with imprisonment until he shall have repaid by labour the value of the advance (Article 228).

On December 6, 1928, the Native Labour Code was promulgated; its essential features are: freedom of labour, obligation to work, establishment of minimum wages, time-limit for contracts, pensions, insurance regarding health and industrial accidents, recruiting methods, compulsory repatriation, payment of deferred wages on repatriation, prohibition of all punishment of natives by private persons, and the restriction of forced labour by the authorities to public purposes only, for which sanction must be sought from Lisbon. The Order of April 11, 1930, required payment of all labour for State purposes, improved living conditions of labourers, and increased the resources of the Protector of Natives. The Orders of July 1930 established additional rights to compensation and pension, and prohibited the sale of alcohol to labourers.

The Colonial Act of July 1930 forms a sort of colonial constitution, of which the second chapter is devoted to native interests. It guarantees immunity for native property from inclusion in land concessions; prohibits officials from exercising any sort of compulsion in aid of recruiting, and limits their intervention to cases of labour for public interests, or in pursuance of judicial, penal, or fiscal decisions.

Special Laws relating to certain Colonies.

In Moçambique labour recruiting for the Transvaal was regulated by Decree of the Royal Commissioner, November 18, 1897, and by the Conventions of 1901, 1908, and 1928; these provide special conditions for recruiting, limit the numbers, regulate the payment of deferred wages, and arrange for Portuguese supervisors in the Transvaal to ensure proper conditions of employment.

The *Prazo System* of Moçambique deserves reference, though now obsolete. It consisted of the leasing by the State of certain areas to private companies, in return for an annual rent. The

Company then undertook police and administrative duties, including the collection of tax; recruitment of labour naturally formed one of the functions of the Company. This system was abolished and re-established at various dates from 1832 onwards, until the introduction of the Labour Code of 1928 put an end to the exclusive rights or interests of any individual in labour recruiting; this was brought into force by Order 118 of September 4, 1930, after a preparatory period of one year previously.

The *identification of natives* is dealt with by Chapter 4 of this Order, which makes the possession of an identity book obligatory for adult males (*caderneta de identificação e trabalho*); it also requires all employers to provide each employee with monthly labour cards (*cartões mensais de trabalho*) on which days of work performed must be indicated by a punch.

There is a Convention with Southern Rhodesia regarding the recruiting of natives (March 6, 1926. For particulars, see 'Southern Rhodesia') and a *modus vivendi* with the island of San Thomé regulating recruiting for employment there (Decree No. 11491/2 of March 9, 1926). There were formerly agreements with France for workers in Madagascar and Réunion.

A local native custom is reported to exist, whereby debts are paid by labour, the debtor undertaking to work without wages for the creditor, the latter having to feed and clothe him meanwhile. The creditor's rights are not transferable, and the system is not economical; it has fallen into disuse.

In 1926 the Direction of Agricultural Services furnished 126,117 labourers to private persons (*Boletim da Agencia geral das Colonias*, December 1927, p. 170). These activities presumably ceased on the introduction of the Labour Code in 1930.

In Angola, Decrees No. 40 and 41 of August 3, 1921, finally abolished forced labour for private persons, and provided that wages for forced labour for public purposes must be at the current rate for private employment.

A circular from the High Commissioner, dated October 2, 1921, emphasizes the duty of the Administration to encourage recruiting with zeal; it advises employers who have insufficient labour to apply to officials of their district; it instructs administrative authorities to see that at least 15 per cent. of the able-bodied males of their districts go to work.

The Native Labour Code was brought into force by Colonial

Decree No. 72 of January 26, 1929; this put an end to all recruiting by officials.

Conditions in *Domestic Service* were regulated by Decree No. 248 of January 22, 1930, which guaranteed complete freedom of occupation.

Deposit by Employers of *Deferred Wages* was facilitated by Decree No. 148 of October 15, 1930.

Extra-territorial recruiting was penalized by Decree No. 219 of February 2, 1930.

Porterage was regulated by Orders No. 36 of February 25, 1922, and No. 148 of August 6, 1923. It is claimed that porterage is now virtually non-existent, owing to the construction of 40,000 kilometres of road.

In San Thomé and Principe Islands, the Native Labour Code was put into force by the Order of April 11, 1930. All unpaid labour is prohibited; detailed regulations are given regarding health, housing, food, wages, hours of work, transport, and repatriation. The statistical department of the Protector of Natives is strengthened; compensation for sickness is elaborated.

In Portuguese Guinea the Regulations for Native Labour of 1923 guarantee the natives against abuses, fix wages, provide for medical attention, and prohibit recruiting by the authorities. In 1927, *contracts* were required for all natives employed in agriculture or industry.

The Native Labour Code was brought into force by Order No. 98 of December 24, 1929.

THE limited development of these countries has apparently so far rendered labour questions of no great importance; details of arrangements are not easily obtainable. Regulations are published in the official Bulletin of Fernando Po, which is not obtainable in Madrid. The following summary appears to represent the existing position.

Forced labour is resorted to by Governor's proclamation, in exceptional circumstances, for purposes of public benefit only; all the inhabitants, both European and African, are liable for work, but substitutes in labour or money are accepted.

Contracts. These extend up to two years; they are compulsory, and are completed before the Protector of Natives (Curador).

Recruiting. Private labour agents are prohibited; the Curador may undertake recruiting in agreement with native chiefs.

Welfare measures are the concern of the Curador.

Medical inspection is compulsory on recruitment.

Punishments are administered by award of the Courts; the employer has no right to inflict these.

Care of Workmen. Employees have the right to hospital treatment at the expense of the employer.

Women and Children. The employment of children below the age of ten is prohibited. Women are restricted to light work, and pregnant women and nursing mothers must be exempted.

Diet Scale. The following were introduced by Decree of the Governor General of the Gulf of Guinea, December 14 and 15, 1927.

Article.		(Grammes per diem.) Scale A.	Scale B.	Scale C.	Scale D.
Rice . . .	.	600	400	500	500
Salt fish . . .	.	200	..	..	100
Palm oil . . .	.	90	80	75	90
Fresh or salt meat .	.	..	100	200	..
Dried beans . .	.	..	200	..	150

with a minimum of four bananas daily, for all diets.

Emancipated Natives (Los indígenas emancipados). These people appear to be detribalized and educated natives who have obtained

Spanish citizenship; they are described as being mainly function-aries or farmers; there are said to be only eighteen in the whole of Spanish Guinea.

Native Welfare Board. The principal measure for promoting the welfare of the native population, as a whole, is the Royal Ordinance, No. 1501 of July 7, 1928, which established a Native Welfare Board to deal with all the territories bordering on the Gulf of Guinea which are under Spanish control. Its objects are to promote the education and the moral and physical welfare of the natives, more particularly those who are not emancipated; to facilitate this advance, in the case of natives able to manage by themselves their own persons and property ('acordar las emanci-paciones de aquellos indígenas capacitados para regir por si mismos sus personas y bienes') and to supervise the management of labour ('intervenir en la reglamentación del trabajo en la forma establecida actualmente, o según aconsejan las circunstancias')

The President is to be the Bishop, Vicar Capitular of the Colony, with a secretary, and six *de jure* and four elective members. Special funds are provided for the Board, and its powers and activities on behalf of the natives are detailed. Half-wages of any contract worker are to be paid to the Board, to be held on trust for the workers. Employers or labourers may appeal from decisions of the Curador of Natives, to the Board; in case of doubt, the decision of the Governor-General is final.

(NOTE. The whole position as regards labour is said to be now under review, in consequence of the obligations accepted by Spain under the Draft International Conventions.)

PART III

INTERNATIONAL DRAFT CONVENTIONS

(NOTE. The following summary is reproduced from the pamphlet printed at Geneva for the League of Nations Association of the United States of America. The subsequent Table of Applications is furnished from information supplied by the International Labour Office at Geneva.)

EXPLANATORY NOTE

THE International Labour Organization was established by the Treaty of Versailles at the close of the Great War. It was created for the purpose of improving the conditions of labour in all countries in the belief that we cannot maintain peace without social justice. Fifty-five nations have become Members—that is to say, nearly all the nations of the world. Of the larger nations only two have failed to join—Russia and the United States.

At least once a year, usually in June, the Organization holds a Conference of representatives of all Member nations to agree upon minimum standards for working conditions and measures for the protection of workers. The minimum standards for working conditions are not intended to reduce industrial practice in all countries to one common level. It is especially provided that they shall not lower any standards already established. The standards so far adopted have indicated a limit to the working day, a minimum age for the employment of children, &c. The measures for the general protection of workers have included the provision of public employment offices, insurance against accident and disease, safety measures, &c.

Each Member country sends to the International Labour Conference four representatives, two to speak for its Government, one for its employers, and one for its employees.

A *draft convention* formulates a minimum standard which a two-thirds majority of the delegates at the Conference believe that the nations of the world can and should observe.

The sovereign States which are Members of the Organization cannot be bound by the action of the Conference, but each State pledges itself to refer the decisions of the Conference to the branch of its government competent to deal with them.

When a country is willing to observe the requirements of a draft convention, it must take legislative or other measures to ensure the observance of these requirements and must notify the Secretary-General of the League of Nations that it undertakes to abide by the convention. As soon as such notification has been given by, as a general rule, two countries, the provisions of the 'draft convention' come into effect as a 'convention' or treaty between those countries that notify their intention to abide by its terms. It is because the proposals of the Conference are to become treaties between nations that they are spoken of as 'draft' conventions. The action of a country in adopting the convention is spoken of as 'ratification'.

Each convention includes a statement that States can take steps to withdraw from the treaty after a period of years—usually ten. Every country must report annually on the measures it has taken to put in force each convention which it has ratified, and a summary of these reports goes to the annual Conference in printed form. At least once in ten years a special report must be made to the Conference on the way the convention is working in the various countries, and the Conference may be asked to consider changing the provisions of the convention. In cases where complaints are made with regard to the non-observance by any State of the provisions of any convention it has ratified, provision is made for a system of inquiry leading ultimately, if necessary, to the submission of the question to the Permanent Court of International Justice.

The International Labour Conference has, up to date, adopted or endorsed thirty-four draft conventions.

The Wording of the Summaries.

In these summaries, no attempt is made to use the exact words of draft conventions. The full text of all the draft conventions can be had from the International Labour Office, Geneva, Switzerland.

The Action of Member Countries.

The International Labour Office publishes every month a chart showing, up to date, the action of each Member country on each of the conventions.

INDEX BY SUBJECTS

Conventions by number, in order of adoption.

LIST OF DRAFT CONVENTIONS

1. The Eight-Hour Day and Forty-eight Hour Week in Industry.
2. Unemployment.
3. Employment of Women before and after Childbirth.
4. Employment of Women during the Night.
5. Age at which Children may be Employed in Industry.
6. Night Work of Young Persons.
7. Berne Convention on the Prohibition of the Use of White Phosphorus in the Manufacture of Matches.[1]
8. Age at which Children may be Employed at Sea.
9. Unemployment Indemnity for Shipwrecked Sailors.
10. Employment Agencies for Seamen.
11. Employment of Children in Agriculture.
12. Right of Agricultural Workers to Organize.
13. Workmen's Compensation in Agriculture.
14. Prohibition of the Use of White Lead in Painting.
15. Weekly Day of Rest for Industrial Workers.
16. Minimum Age for Trimmers and Stokers.
17. Compulsory Medical Examination of Young Persons Employed at Sea.
18. Workmen's Compensation for Industrial Accidents.
19. Workmen's Compensation for Occupational Diseases.
20. Compensation of Workmen of Foreign Citizenship.
21. Prohibition of Night Work in Bakeries.
22. Simplification of Inspection of Emigrants on Board Ship.
23. Seamen's Articles of Agreement.
24. Repatriation of Seamen.
25. Sickness Insurance for Workers in Industry and Commerce, and for Domestic Servants.
26. Sickness Insurance for Agricultural Workers.
27. Creation of Minimum Wage Fixing Machinery.
28. Marking of the Weight on Heavy Packages transported by Vessels.
29. Protection against Accidents of Workers employed in Loading or Unloading Ships.
30. Forced or Compulsory Labour.
31. The Regulation of Hours of Work in Commerce and Offices.
32. Hours of Work in Mines.
33. Age of admission to Non-industrial Occupations.
34. Revised convention concerning the protection against accidents of workers employed in loading or unloading ships.

[1] This Convention of 1906 was commended to States by a Recommendation of the Conference and thus revived.

CONVENTIONS

First Session (*Washington*, 1919)

1. Draft Convention concerning the EIGHT-HOUR DAY AND FORTY-EIGHT-HOUR WEEK IN INDUSTRY.

The working day in INDUSTRY is not to be more than *eight hours* long and the working week is not to consist of more than *forty-eight hours*, except in the following cases:

(1) *Managerial, supervisory*, or *confidential* work.

(2) Under certain *sanctions* when the hours on one or more days of the week are *less than eight*.

(3) Adjustments under a *shift system* if the average number of hours over a period of three weeks or less does not exceed eight per day and forty-eight per week.

(4) *Accident* or *emergency* or in case of *force majeure* in order to avoid serious interference with the ordinary working of the undertaking.

(5) In *continuous processes* under a shift system if the hours do not average more than fifty-six in the week, and any legal provision for rest days is observed.

(6) By *agreement*, in exceptional cases, between the *workers'* and *employers' organizations* with the *consent* of the *Government*, if the average weekly hours over the period covered by the agreement do not exceed forty-eight.

(7) *Preparatory, complementary*, and *intermittent* work, and *exceptional cases* of pressure of work for which Government *regulation* issued after consultation with the organizations of employers and workers concerned may grant *temporary* or *permanent exceptions* with the proviso that the rate of pay for overtime be not less than one and one-quarter times the regular rate.

(8) A sliding scale of applications for *Japan*, postponed application for *Greece* and *Rumania*, a ten-hour limit for *India*, postponement of all regulation for *China, Persia*, and *Siam*.

This Convention is to apply to all work done in factories, mines, and quarries, power-houses, construction work, transport by land, &c., but not to commerce or agriculture. Each country is to make its own definitions of commerce and agriculture. It does not apply to establishments in which only members of the same family are employed.

2. Draft Convention concerning UNEMPLOYMENT.

Governments are to establish *free public employment offices.*

These are to be conducted under advice from committees on which employers and employees are represented. Private agencies are to be co-ordinated with the public system. As far as may be found possible, the various national systems are to be co-ordinated through the International Labour Office, in agreement with the countries concerned.

Each Member country is to send to the International Labour Office at least once every three months, all available information on the unemployment and the means it is using to decrease it.

If a State has an unemployment insurance system it is to treat workers from other countries which have accepted the Convention in the same way as its own workers, provided that an agreement to that effect can be made.

3. Draft Convention concerning THE EMPLOYMENT OF WOMEN BEFORE AND AFTER CHILDBIRTH.

A woman is not to be employed in industrial or commercial work for six weeks after confinement; she shall be free to leave such work six weeks before confinement; and she shall not be discharged during the period of absence. And should sickness due to her condition supervene, during such further period as may be fixed by the competent authority in each country. During the time she is not working she is to draw relief or insurance from Public funds sufficient to support herself and her baby, and to receive free medical attendance. When she returns to work she is to be allowed half an hour twice a day, during working hours, to nurse her child.

These provisions do not apply to agricultural employment, and each Government is to make its own definition of agriculture. Family undertakings are also excepted.

4. Draft Convention concerning THE EMPLOYMENT OF WOMEN IN INDUSTRY DURING THE NIGHT.

A woman is not to be employed in industry at night except in an undertaking in which only her family is employed.

Each country is to make its own *definition of the night period,* with the understanding that it is to cover eleven consecutive hours, including the periods between 10 p.m. and 5 a.m.

The rule is subject to *limited exceptions* with respect to:
(1) *emergencies* and cases of *force majeure* leading to interruption of work;

(2) work on *perishable materials*;

(3) *seasonal* work;

(4) adjustments to *climatic conditions*;

(5) conditions in *India* and *Siam*.

5. Draft Convention concerning THE AGE AT WHICH CHILDREN MAY BE EMPLOYED IN INDUSTRY.

Children are not to be employed in industrial work before they are *fourteen*.

This prohibition applies to work in factories, mines and quarries, power-houses, construction, transportation, &c., but it does not apply to agriculture and commerce. Each country is to decide for itself what it will consider agriculture and commerce. It does not apply to family undertakings or approved technical schools. To aid enforcement a register showing the ages of juveniles under 16 must be kept in industrial undertakings. Special provisions are included for Japan and India.

6. Draft Convention concerning NIGHT WORK OF YOUNG PERSONS.

No one under eighteen is to be employed *in industry during the night* except in an undertaking in which only members of the same family are employed and in certain industries where processes must be continuous.

This prohibition applies to factories, mines and quarries, power-houses, construction, transportation, &c., but not to commerce and agriculture. Each country is to decide for itself what it will consider commerce and agriculture. Each country is also to make its own definition of 'night', with the understanding that it shall name a period covering at least eleven consecutive hours and including the time between 10 p.m. and 5 a.m.

Limited *exceptions* are allowed with respect to:

(1) certain industries which must work continuously day and night (for young persons over the age of 16);

(2) the definition of 'night' in *certain industries* and in *tropical countries*;

(3) *emergencies* (for young persons between the ages of 16 and 18);

(4) certain conditions in *Japan* and *India*;

(5) coal and lignite mines (no age specified) if an interval ordinarily of 15 hours and never of less than 13 hours separates two work periods.

7. Berne Convention concerning THE PROHIBITION OF THE USE OF WHITE PHOSPHORUS IN THE MANUFACTURE OF MATCHES.

This Convention was prepared by the International Association for Labour Legislation and signed at Berne on September 26, 1906. The International Labour Conference adopted at its First Session a Recommendation in favour of the ratification of the Convention, which lays down that countries are to forbid the *manufacture, importation,* and *sale* of *matches* containing *white (yellow) phosphorus.*

Second Session (Genoa, 1920)

8. Draft Convention concerning AGE AT WHICH CHILDREN MAY BE EMPLOYED AT SEA.

Children under fourteen are not to be employed on vessels.

This does not apply to properly supervised school ships, or vessels on which only members of the same family are employed.

9. Draft Convention concerning UNEMPLOYMENT INDEMNITY FOR SHIPWRECKED SAILORS.

In case of *wreck*, seamen are to receive *wages* from their employers, while they are without employment, up to a period of two months.

10. Draft Convention concerning EMPLOYMENT AGENCIES FOR SEAMEN.

Every country is to have *free employment offices for seamen.*

These may be maintained either by employers and seamen acting together, or by the State, under advice from joint committees of employers and seamen. Where agencies of different types exist, steps are to be taken to co-ordinate them on a national basis.

Private employment agencies for seamen are to be abolished. (Existing agencies may be allowed to continue temporarily under Government licence and supervision.)

Freedom of choice of ship is assured to seamen, and of crew to the shipowner, opportunity is assured to seamen for examining contracts before and after signing, and access to employment agencies by seamen of all ratifying countries where industrial conditions are in general the same. Ratifying countries are to report to the International Labour Office statistical and other information concerning unemployment among seamen and the work of employment agencies.

Third Session (Geneva, 1921)

11. Draft Convention concerning EMPLOYMENT OF CHILDREN IN AGRICULTURE.

Children *under fourteen* are not to be employed in agriculture in any way that will *interfere with their school work.*

12. Draft Convention concerning THE RIGHT OF AGRICULTURAL WORKERS TO ORGANIZE.

The *agricultural workers* of any country are to have the same *right to organize* as have its *industrial workers.*

13. Draft Convention concerning WORKMEN'S COMPENSATION IN AGRICULTURE.

Agricultural workers are to be included in the operation of *workmen's compensation* laws.

14. Draft Convention concerning PROHIBITION OF THE USE OF WHITE LEAD IN PAINTING.

White lead is *not to be used* in the *internal* painting of buildings, *except* in certain circumstances enumerated in the Convention.

The steps to be taken to prevent lead-poisoning when white lead may be used are also laid down. The employment of women and children in lead-painting work is completely prohibited.

15. Draft Convention concerning A WEEKLY DAY OF REST FOR INDUSTRIAL WORKERS.

Every Member of the staff of every *industrial undertaking* is to have a *weekly rest* period of twenty-four consecutive hours. As far as possible this rest day is to be the general day of rest (e.g. Sunday).

The Convention applies to factories, mines and quarries, powerhouses, construction, transportation, &c., but not agriculture and commerce. Each country is to make its own definition of agriculture and commerce.

16. Draft Convention concerning THE MINIMUM AGE FOR TRIMMERS AND STOKERS.

No one *under eighteen* is to work on a vessel as *trimmer* or *stoker.*
Exceptions are provided for in the case of:
(1) *school ships;*
(2) vessels mainly propelled by *other means* than *steam;*

(3) The *coastal* trade of *India* and *Japan*;

(4) impossibility of obtaining a worker over eighteen, when two boys of sixteen or over may be employed in his place.

17. Draft Convention concerning COMPULSORY MEDICAL EXAMINATION OF YOUNG PERSONS EMPLOYED AT SEA.

Any one *under eighteen* wishing to work on a vessel must have, each year, a properly authenticated *medical certificate* declaring him fit for the work. Temporary exceptions are allowed in certain emergencies.

Fourth, Fifth, and Sixth Sessions (*Geneva*, 1922, 1923, *and* 1924)

Because the Conventions adopted by the first three Sessions of the Conference had required the legislative bodies or other competent authorities of the Member countries to consider an extensive programme of labour legislation, it was judged best to give them time to act before pressing them with further proposals; therefore the Fourth, Fifth, and Sixth Sessions adopted only Recommendations.

Seventh Session (*Geneva*, 1925)

18. Draft Convention concerning WORKMEN'S COMPENSATION FOR INDUSTRIAL ACCIDENTS.

Workmen (or, if the accident is fatal, their dependants) are to receive *compensation* for industrial *accidents*.

Compensation is payable as from the fifth day after the accident, and injured workmen are also entitled to medical and surgical services, medicines, artificial limbs, and surgical appliances. In cases of permanent incapacity or death the compensation is to be paid, as a general rule, in the form of a pension.

The Government of each country is to see to it that employers carry safe and sufficient insurance to cover such costs.

This *does not apply* to seamen and fishermen (for whom provision is to be made by a later Convention) or to persons covered by some special scheme giving equal or superior benefits. On the question of agriculture, see Convention 13. Exception may be made in the case of casual workers, out-workers, members of the employer's family, and non-manual workers receiving remuneration above a limit to be fixed by national law.

19. Draft Convention concerning WORKMEN'S COMPENSATIONS FOR OCCUPATIONAL DISEASES.

Workmen are to be *compensated* for *occupational diseases* on the same principles as for industrial accidents. The rates of compensation shall not be less than those for industrial accidents.

(The Convention gives a provisional list of occupational diseases.)

20. Draft Convention concerning COMPENSATION OF WORKMEN OF FOREIGN CITIZENSHIP.

Citizens of any *country ratifying* this Convention, if injured while at work in another ratifying country, are to receive *accident compensation* on the same terms as would citizens of the country in which the accident occurred.

21. Draft Convention concerning PROHIBITION OF NIGHT WORK IN BAKERIES.

Night work in bakeries is *forbidden*.

Except under certain stipulated conditions, the 'night' shall cover seven hours, including the period between 11 p.m. and 5 a.m. Wholesale manufacture of biscuits is excepted, and there is provision for limited exceptions, after consultation with the employers' and workers' organizations concerned, for—

(1) *preparatory* or *complementary* work;
(2) conditions in *tropical* countries;
(3) arrangement of the *weekly rest*;
(4) *emergencies*.

Eighth Session (Geneva, 1926)

22. Draft Convention concerning SIMPLIFICATION OF INSPECTION OF EMIGRANTS ON BOARD SHIP.

This Convention lays down the principle that *inspectors* of *emigrants* on board an emigrant ship are not to be appointed *by more than one Government*, which, except an agreement be made to the contrary, is to be the Government of the flag flown by the ship.

(This is not to prevent any Government from sending an observer to accompany emigrants.)

Ninth Session (Geneva, 1926)

23. Draft Convention concerning SEAMEN'S ARTICLES OF AGREEMENT.

Seamen's articles of agreement are to be signed by both parties, under *public supervision*, and with certainty that the *seaman understands* their content. They are to contain a clear statement of the rights and obligations of each party as called for in detailed provisions of the Convention. Seamen, on leaving a ship, shall be provided with a record of their service which shall not contain any statement as to the quality of their work or as to their wages.

24. Draft Convention concerning REPATRIATION OF SEAMEN.

Seamen are not to be left in a foreign country without arrangements for *getting back* either to *their own country*, or to the port at which they were engaged or to the port from which the voyage commenced.

Special arrangements are stipulated for sailors who must be left behind on account of illness or discharge for which they had no responsibility, for foreign seamen engaged in a country other than their own, &c.

Tenth Session (Geneva, 1927)

25. Draft Convention concerning SICKNESS INSURANCE FOR WORKERS IN INDUSTRY AND COMMERCE, AND DOMESTIC SERVANTS.

Sickness insurance under *public control* is to be *compulsory* for all workers except those exempted in the terms of the Convention.

Among the *exceptions* are agricultural workers, provided for in Convention 26; seamen and sea-fishermen for whom provision 'may be made by decision of a later Session of the Conference'; workers whose wages are above a figure to be named by each country; workers below or above the normal ages of self-support; members of employers' families, &c.

Member States may suspend the application of the Convention in very thinly populated areas, but Finland is the only European State whose conditions are considered to justify this suspension.

Any one incapable of work because of an abnormal bodily or mental condition is to receive cash benefits calculated from not more than three days after he is officially recognized as ill. He is to receive these benefits for at least twenty-six weeks if he continues unable to work, and during this time is to be entitled to the services of a doctor and to medicines and appliances.

The insurance must be administered by self-governing insurance agencies, which may be either governmental or private, but must not be run for profit and must be under Government supervision.

26. Draft Convention concerning SICKNESS INSURANCE FOR AGRICULTURAL WORKERS.

Compulsory sickness insurance is to be provided for all agricultural workers on terms similar to those on which it is provided for industrial and other workers in Convention 25.

Eleventh Session (Geneva, 1928)

27. Draft Convention concerning FIXING OF MINIMUM WAGE RATES.

Governments are to provide *machinery* for *fixing minimum wage rates* in *manufacturing* and *commercial* trades wherever no arrangements exist for effective regulation of wages, by collective bargaining or otherwise, and existing wage rates are exceptionally low. This applies especially to home working trades. The Governments are to decide where this machinery is to be applied.

Such machinery is to be applied only after *consultation* with representatives of *employers* and *workers* concerned, including representatives of their respective organizations where such exist. Employers and workers shall be associated in the operation of wage-fixing machinery and in *equal* numbers.

Each Member Government shall *report annually* to the International Labour Office on the trades in which minimum wage rates have been established, the methods and results, the approximate number of workers covered, the rates fixed, &c.

Twelfth Session (Geneva, 1929)

28. Draft Convention concerning THE MARKING OF THE WEIGHT ON HEAVY PACKAGES TRANSPORTED BY VESSELS.

Any *package* or *object* of *one thousand kilograms* (one metric ton) or more gross weight consigned within the territory of any Member ratifying the Convention for *transport* by *sea* or *inland waterway* is to have had its *gross weight* durably *marked* on it on the outside before it is loaded on a ship or vessel. The obligation to see that this requirement is observed rests solely upon the Government of the country from which it is consigned.

29. Draft Convention concerning THE PROTECTION AGAINST ACCIDENTS OF WORKERS EMPLOYED IN LOADING OR UNLOADING SHIPS.

The *safety* of workers employed in *loading* and *unloading* ships is to be safeguarded by certain requirements with regard to examination and protection of machinery and electric conductors, the nature and location of ladders, gangways, &c., the stacking and storing of cargo and various specified precautions, generally applicable to *workplaces* and *working arrangements* on docks and ships, by day and night.

Exceptions to the specific provisions are granted when the processes in question are carried on only occasionally or are confined to ships of special classes, or where climatic conditions render them impracticable; such exceptions must be reported to the International Labour Office.

Fourteenth Session (Geneva, 1930)

30. Draft Convention concerning FORCED OR COMPULSORY LABOUR.

Each Member is to *suppress* the use of *forced* or *compulsory* labour in all its forms within the *shortest possible period*, and during that period is to resort to it only for *public purposes* and as an *exceptional measure* subject to certain conditions and guarantees.

Five years after the Convention comes into force the Governing Body of the International Labour Office is to consider the possibility of *suppressing* such labour *without a further transitional period* and the desirability of placing on the agenda of the Conference a proposal for immediate suppression.

Forced or compulsory labour is *defined* as all *work* or service which is *exacted* from any person under the menace of any *penalty* and for which the said person has *not* offered himself *voluntarily*.

The following are specifically exempted from the application of this Convention:

(a) any *military service*;

(b) any work or service which forms part of the *normal civic obligation* of the citizens of a fully self-governing country;

(c) *convict labour* under public supervision and control and not for private profit;

(d) *emergency* service;

(e) minor *communal services*, providing members of the community or their direct representatives have the right to be consulted in regard to the need for such services;

(f) work demanded by law or custom where production is organized *on a communal basis*, and produce or profit accrues to the community.

There is to be *immediate prohibition* of the imposition of forced or compulsory labour:

(a) for *private profit*;

(b) for work *underground* in mines;

(c) on a community as *collective punishment* for crimes committed by any of its members;

For the transitional period measures are detailed guaranteeing:

(a) that such labour be *only* imposed *for public purposes* when it is necessary and *unavoidable*, in the direct interest of the community concerned;

(b) that the imposition of such work as a tax or for the execution of public works by chiefs meet the requirements under (a) and that it will *not entail removal* of workers from their habitual place of residence and will be in accord with the *exigencies* of *religion, social life, and agriculture*;

(c) that only able-bodied *males* of an approximate age between 18 and 45 be called on for such labour, with certain precautions as to health, exemptions, and family and social life;

(d) that the working day and week, the *periods* for which such labour is exacted and the *frequency* of exaction, do not exceed certain limits (maximum period: 60 days in the year);

(e) that *remuneration* be at the same rates as for similar labour voluntarily undertaken, and be safeguarded by certain regulations with respect to payment;

(f) that the *health* of workers and their *repatriation* at the end of service be provided for in stipulated ways;

(g) that provision be made to insure *subsistence of workers' families*, especially facilities for the remittance of a portion of the workers' wages.

Detailed arrangements are made for the *enforcement* of the provisions of the Convention.

31. Draft Convention concerning REGULATION OF HOURS OF WORK IN COMMERCE AND OFFICES.

The working day in commerce and offices is not to be more than *eight hours* long and the working week is not to consist of more than *forty-eight hours* except under the following conditions:

1. Hours of work in a day may exceed eight, but not exceed ten:

(a) If *weekly hours* do not exceed forty-eight;

(b) *To make up hours lost* by a general interruption of work due to *holidays*, or *force majeure*—if the time lost is made up within a reasonable time—on not more than thirty days in one year and if not more than one hour be added to any day. Certain adjustments of these provisions are allowed the enforcing authorities.

2. The enforcing authority may declare exceptions which are allowable *permanently for:*

(a) inherently *intermittent* work (caretakers, &c.);

(b) *preparatory* or *complementary* work;

(c) any establishment where the nature of the work, size of population, or the number of persons employed makes the *limits inapplicable* temporarily for :

(i) actual or threatened *accident* or *force majeure.*

(ii) to prevent loss of *perishable* goods or danger to *technical* results;

(iii) *special work*, such as stock-taking, &c.;

(iv) *abnormal pressure* of work with which employer cannot ordinarily be expected to deal by other means.

The number of additional hours per day and, in respect of temporary exceptions, in the year shall be regulated and the *rate of pay* (except in the case of accident) shall not be less than *one and a half times the regular rate.* The regulation shall be made after consultation with employers' and workers' organizations concerned, special attention being paid to collective agreements, if any.

The provisions may be suspended in the case of emergency endangering *national safety.*

Nothing in the Convention shall affect any custom or agreement providing shorter *hours* or *higher remuneration.*

Provisions for *enforcement* are stipulated.

Fifteenth Session (Geneva, 1931)

32. Draft Convention concerning HOURS OF WORK IN MINES. Fixes hours of work at 7¾ from bank to bank.

Sixteenth Session (Geneva, 1932)

33. Draft Convention concerning AGE OF ADMISSION TO NON-INDUSTRIAL OCCUPATIONS.

A general minimum age is fixed at 14 years or the school-leaving age, whichever is the higher. Subject to specified safeguards light work may be authorized for children over twelve.

34. Revised Convention concerning THE PROTECTION AGAINST ACCIDENTS OF WORKERS EMPLOYED IN LOADING OR UNLOADING SHIPS.

Embodies technical amendments to the 1929 Convention.

Article 421

'The members engage to apply conventions which they have ratified in accordance with the provisions of this part of the present Treaty to their colonies, protectorates, and possessions which are not fully self-governing:

(1) Except where owing to the local conditions the convention is inapplicable, or

(2) Subject to such modifications as may be necessary to adapt the Convention to local conditions.

And each of the Members shall notify to the International Labour Office the action taken in respect of each of its colonies, protectorates, and possessions which are not fully self-governing.

THE APPLICATION OF INTERNATIONAL LABOUR CONVENTIONS IN AFRICA

NOTE. In many instances where various powers are shown as not having applied conventions, they nevertheless have existing legislation in their colonies which largely meets the requirements of the conventions.

Convention	Ratification by African Colonial Power	Legislative application in African Territories
1. Hours	Belgium	Not applied.
2. Unemployment	Belgium	,,
	France	,,
	Great Britain	,,
	Italy	,,
	South Africa	Applied in the Union.
	Spain	Applied in Rio de Oro and Spanish Guinea.
3. Childbirth	Spain	Applied in Rio de Oro and Spanish Guinea.
4. Night work, women	Belgium	Applied in Belgian Congo and Ruanda-Urundi.
	France	Not applied.
	Great Britain	Applied in Gold Coast, Nigeria, Uganda, Zanzibar.
	Italy	Not applied.
	South Africa	Applied in the Union.
5. Minimum age, industry	Belgium	Not applied.
	Great Britain	Partly applied in Gambia, Gold Coast, Kenya, Nigeria, Sierra Leone, Sudan, Tanganyika, Uganda, Zanzibar.
6. Night work, young persons	Belgium	Not applied.
	France	,,
	Great Britain	Applied in Nigeria and Zanzibar; partly applied in Uganda.
	Italy	Not applied.
7. Prohibition of White Phosphorus in matches	(Berne Convention of 1906)	

Convention	Ratification by African Colonial Power	Legislative application in African Territories
8. Minimum age, sea	Belgium	Not applied.
	Great Britain	Applied in Zanzibar; partly applied in Gold Coast and Sierra Leone.
	Spain	Applied in Rio de Oro and Spanish Guinea.
9. Unemployment indemnity	Belgium	Not applied.
	France	,,
	Great Britain	,,
	Italy	,,
	Spain	Applied in Rio de Oro and Spanish Guinea.
10. Employment for seamen	Belgium	Not applied.
	France	Applied in Algeria and Tunisia.
	Italy	Not applied.
11. Minimum age in agriculture	Belgium	Not applied.
	Italy	,,
12. Right of association, agriculture	Belgium	Not applied.
	France	Applied in Algeria.
	Great Britain	Applied in all territories.
	Italy	Not applied.
13. Workmen's compensation, agriculture	France	Applied in Algeria.
	Great Britain	Applied in Nigeria, N. Rhodesia, Tanganyika, Somaliland.
14. White lead	Belgium	Not applied.
	France	Applied in Algeria, Morocco.
	Spain	Applied in Rio de Oro and Spanish Guinea.
15. Weekly rest	Belgium	Not applied.
	France	,,
	Italy	Observed in practice.
	Portugal	Not applied.
	Spain	Applied in Rio de Oro and Spanish Guinea.

Convention	Ratification by African Colonial Power	Legislative application in African Territories
16. Minimum age, trimmers and stokers	Belgium	Not applied.
	France	Applied in Algeria, Morocco.
	Great Britain	Partial provision exists in Gambia, Gold Coast, Kenya, Nigeria, Sierra Leone, and Tanganyika.
	Italy	Not applied.
	Spain	Applied in Rio de Oro and Spanish Guinea.
17. Medical examination, young persons employed at sea	Belgium	Not applied.
	France	Applied in Algeria.
	Great Britain	Partial provision exists in Gambia, Gold Coast, Kenya, Nigeria, Sierra Leone, and Tanganyika.
	Italy	Not applied.
	Spain	Applied in Rio de Oro and Spanish Guinea.
18. Workmen's compensation, accidents	Belgium	Applied in Belgian Congo and Ruanda-Urundi.
	Portugal	Not applied.
	Spain	Applied in Rio de Oro and Spanish Guinea.
19. Workmen's compensation, diseases	Belgium	Applied in Belgian Congo and Ruanda-Urundi.
	Great Britain	Partly applied in N. Rhodesia.
	Portugal	Not applied.
20. Equality of treatment, accidents	Belgium	Not applied.
	France	Applied in Algeria, Morocco, and Tunisia.
	Great Britain	Applied in Kenya, Nigeria, N. Rhodesia, Sierra Leone, Somaliland, Tanganyika, and Uganda.
	Italy	Applied in Eritrea, Tripolitania, and Cyrenaica.
	Portugal	Not applied.
	South Africa	Applied in Union.

Convention	Ratification by African Colonial Power	Legislative application in African territories
21. Night work in bakeries.		
22. Inspection of emigrants on board ship	Belgium	Not applied.
23. Seamen's articles of agreement	Belgium	Not applied.
	France	Applied in Algeria.
	Italy	Applied in Eritrea and Somaliland.
	Spain	Applied in Rio de Oro and Spanish Guinea.
24. Repatriation of seamen	Belgium	Not applied.
	France	Applied in Algeria, Tunisia.
	Italy	Applied in all colonies.
25 and 26. Sickness insurance, industry and agriculture	Great Britain	Not applied.
27. Minimum wage-fixing machinery	France	Not applied.
	Great Britain	Kenya, Nigeria.
	Italy	Not applied.
	Spain	Applied in Rio de Oro and Spanish Guinea.
28. Weight of packages	Portugal	Not applied.
29. Dockers		
30. Forced Labour	Great Britain.	Applied in all territories.
	Liberia	Applied.
	Spain	Applied in all territories.
31. Hours of work in commerce.		
32. Hours of work in mines.		
33. Age of Admission: non-industrial occupations.		
34. Accidents in loading or unloading ships.		

INDEX

Note.—In this index the page figures referring to general subjects are in roman type; those to legislation in *italic* type; those to Draft Conventions in **clarendon** type.